PA

MW01135339

W H E N
NOVEMBER
C O M E S

Becka

BAILEY

Pacific Press Publishing Association
Boise, Idaho
Oshawa, Ontario, Canada

Most names of characters and a few names of places in this story have been changed.

Edited by Marvin Moore
Designed by Dennis Ferree
Cover art by Mark Cable
Typeset in 10/12 Century Schoolbook

Library of Congress Cataloging-in-Publication Data
Montgomery, Paula.
    When November comes / Paula Montgomery.
        p.   cm. — (The Beck Bailey series: bk. 4)
    Summary: Becka spends the summer as a counselor at a church camp in Texas where she falls in love with one of the male counselors.
    ISBN 0-8163-1033-5
    1. Church camps—Seventh-day Adventists—Juvenile literature. 2. Camp counselors—Juvenile literature. [1. Church camps. 2. Camps. 3. Christian life.] I. Title. II. Series: Montgomery, Paula. Becka Bailey Series; bk. 4.
BV1650.M624   1991
259'.8—dc20   90-22703
                                                                              CIP
                                                                               AC

91 92 93 94 95 • 5 4 3 2 1

Contents

To Rhett,
for your amusing counsel
and gentle prodding.

Chapter 1

El Camino Ranch

On an edge of the wild and wind-swept desert Southwest rose a hilly oasis, clumps of Spanish oak and cedar, juniper and pecan trees. The trees were dwarfed by too little rain under a mulish, hot sun. A narrow road ribboned its way among those hills, entwining modern bunkhouses—cabins that peeked here and there from the greenery of El Camino Ranch. At the top of the hill stood a large conference hall that also doubled as a recreation room and cafeteria.

In one of the cabins Becka Bailey floundered, caught in a nightmare. She dreamed she was tumbling over and over in a cactus bed, its needles glowing like tiny branding irons, piercing her arms, face, neck . . .

"Aayeee!" she screamed, waking abruptly to burning skin. She squinted in the twilight at her nightshirt that looked peppered with busy red blurs. "Ants!" she gasped and leapt from her bunk, shaking the creatures from her hair. Frantically, she brushed them off, then raced to the sink for her contact lenses.

"If I could just see," she gurgled into the water that splashed soothingly against her fiery face. With her nose nearly touching the reflection in the mirror, Becka groaned at the puffy image staring back at her.

"I must be allergic to those stupid creatures," she thought in disgust. "First my scalp gets sunburned, then I break out in heat rash, and now I'm swelling up with ant stings. What next?"

She half-grinned at her sorry reflection. "Don't ask!" it warned.

She could hear her roommate showering in the other bathroom as she tried in vain to put the contact lenses in her swollen eyes. Finally, with a deep sigh, Becka gave up the effort.

"Great! In a few minutes I'm supposed to run the obstacle course, and I can't even see."

She hastily combed her long, blondish hair, then fumbled for the jeans and T-shirt hanging next to her bunk bed. Quickly dressing, she headed for the screen door.

"Good morning!" She heard Tricia's melodic voice as her robed friend emerged from the small, steamy room.

"The morning is not good," Becka retorted. "I've just been attacked by an army of fire ants. Would you believe our room's full of them."

"Oh, no!" Tricia rolled her blue eyes dramatically. "Funny! They didn't bother me." She giggled. "I must not be as sweet as you."

"Well, I don't feel very sweet at the moment," Becka said. "My skin's burning, my eyes are too swollen to wear my contacts, and I'm so near-sighted I can't see beyond a foot."

"Oooo!" Tricia moved closer. "They *are* swollen, and your face is all red—and your arms!" Her voice filled with concern. "If you'll wait a few minutes, I'll help you hike up to the lodge."

"Thanks, but no! I'll manage OK," Becka replied, stepping outside onto the cement porch. She blinked in the dazzling sunlight and gazed around at a blurry world.

"Cauliflower!" she thought. "Everything looks like cauliflower—green, gray, and brown *fuzzy* cauliflower!"

Cautiously, she rounded the side of the cabin toward the path that led up the hill through what she called bushes. Her boyfriend, Bradley Colton, had corrected her their first day at the youth ranch. "These are trees, Becka."

"But trees tower way up into the sky," she protested. "These things barely reach above my head."

Her heart had fluttered a little when he regarded her with obvious amusement. "This is arid land, not the rainy Northwest you're used to. Little rain makes little trees," he had joked, "but trees just the same."

Becka wasn't convinced. They still looked like bushes to her. And right now those bushes seemed to reach out with thorny claws as she struggled awkwardly along, trying to stay on the path.

Just two days before, she had spent hours with other staff members, watching films and relearning how to guide sightless campers around such hilly terrain. Now, in her struggle, she keenly sensed the helplessness blind campers must feel. At least she could see images, however blurred and foreign they looked. What a strange and frightening world darkness would create, surrounded by those prickly branches along the steep, dirt path!

"I'll take extra good care of my blind campers," she vowed, "that is, *if* I can see by then myself—and right now I truly wonder if I ever will."

She sighed again. Whatever was she doing, training as a counselor in this sweltering, forsaken country, when she could have applied instead for a job again at Camp Wautum Woods in the cool Northwest? Two toilsome years of college had passed since that sunny-snowy summer as a camp counselor in the mountains.

Then she spotted the reason for her choosing El Camino Ranch. At least she *thought* the faceless blob—rising like a pillar beside the stone bridge—was Brad.

"Becka!" he called anxiously. "What in the world happened to you?"

"Fire ants!" She shot the words at him like bullets.

"Don't tell me you didn't have ants at Camp Wautum Woods either," he pleaded.

"We had ants," she answered primly, "but they were well-mannered ants. They stayed on the ground where they belonged, and never would one stray thought of stinging a person enter their cute little heads."

Brad chuckled. "I'm sorry, Becka." He took her hand and helped her over the bridge. "Looks like you don't have your contacts in this morning, huh?"

"How'd you ever guess?" Sarcasm coated the statement.

"Better let go of my hand," she warned, "before someone accuses us of public display of affection."

"That rule begins Sunday when our first group of campers arrives," he told her. "Until then I can hold your hand. Anyway, who would argue with my helping a damsel in distress? And a beautiful one at that!"

His soft-spoken phrases made her crankiness flee by the time they had reached the top of the path. There the cafeteria/lodge stood like a mammoth, white-stoned castle. Instead of a mote, an acre of asphalt surrounded it, which served as a parking lot and gathering place for line calls. The lodge, perched atop a high hill, commanded a majestic sweep of lower hills stretching for miles in several directions. And although a sea of low-sprawling trees glittered in the early morning sun, a brown, parched earth slept silently beneath their branches.

When both of them caught their breath, Brad suggested, "Alec and I could ask for permission to enter girls' village after lunch and spray those little pests of yours. After all, Alec wouldn't want Tricia getting stung too. She's pretty special to him, you know."

Becka grinned. "That's quite obvious." She knew that Alec, Brad's best friend, had been dating her roommate, Tricia, even longer than the seven months she and Bradley Colton had been dating.

Just then the camp director, Luke Porter, cleared his throat and spoke above the milling crowd. "Let's head for the obstacle course!"

Becka's squeaky, "But I can't see!" captured his attention at once.

"What happened to your face?" Luke asked. "It looks terribly sunburned or something."

"Fire ants. Can't use my contact lenses," she replied. "My eyelids feel like swollen shoe leather."

"Some people come up with the best excuses to escape running the obstacle course," he muttered good-naturedly. "See the nurse, or return to your cabin until the swelling goes down."

Brad helped Becka back to the bridge. "Are you sure you'll

make it to your cabin all right?" he asked.

"I'm sure." She smiled up at him. "Thanks so much for guiding me to the edge of no man's land."

"For such a beautiful woman, my pleasure," he said. "Now it's off to the obstacle course!"

After he left, Becka picked her way carefully through the trees again, thinking warmly about the nice compliment her boyfriend had just given her, and feeling smug about the long, luxurious shower she would enjoy while her fellow staff members raced through the hills.

The morning before, she had taken great pleasure, though, in racing against Neil Bradberry, who was part of the college recruiting team visiting briefly from her school. She grinned at the memory of him. Neil had looked like a chubby Goliath stuffed into a jogging outfit when he swaggered up to the starting line and blustered, "OK, let's settle this battle between the guys and gals once and for all!" He acted, she thought, as though winning the race would be a snap.

Becka laughed aloud at his confidence, this fellow who had been turning to Jello behind a desk all year, while she had run several miles every morning before classes.

The obstacle course was designed to get the staff into shape before their campers arrived. Becka was thankful that tall Glen Barthlow—"Mr. Military Man," as she called him—was part of her team. Glen, a canoeing instructor, would run ahead of her, pacing her just enough to encourage a faster time each morning.

First, they ran three-quarters of a mile to a wire that they scrambled under. Then they raced downhill, sloshing through a muddy creekbed and scampering up a steep bank and over a wall. Next, a log awaited for them to crawl under, then a massive pile of tires to scale. After that they all took off, yard by flying yard, cross-country through the dewy grass and over the rocky soil, another half-mile, until they reached the edge of a cliff and helped one another down. Next they faced two ropes stretched over a creek. They clung to one and tight-rope-walked across the other. Safely across, they raced uphill and the three-quarters of a mile return to the starting point. To cool down, the groups hiked the mile back to the cafeteria.

Becka couldn't believe how quickly Neil began to pant and puff. As she breezed past him, she felt like twittering, "Oh, Neil! Is this pace fast enough for you?" But her conscience wouldn't allow it.

Stopping to maneuver under the wire, Becka's amusement turned to genuine concern when she spotted Neil dragging his bloated self across the field. His face, already soaked in sweat, blazed scarlet under the warming sun.

"He'll never make it," she breathed, then wondered if a guy that young could suffer a heart attack. Away she flew to the next obstacle and ran so fast she never discovered if Neil had actually completed the entire course or not.

Becka was glad to see that Neil was still alive at breakfast an hour later. She also noted that he was a much meeker and quieter man. He scarcely spoke a word during the entire meal.

After her shower Becka straightened up the cabin, steering clear of the clusters of ants that seemed to multiply by the minute. She hesitated at the window and gazed out at the cloudless sky and fuzzy horizon. How different the Southwest was compared to her mountainous home! She recalled two summers before when Geoffrey Blake had followed her the 2,000 miles to her college, then promptly dumped her for another girl.

"Oh, the unpredictability of infatuation!" she mused, then wondered about Brad. Was this infatuation also? After Geoff she had dated several guys, but none like Brad.

"More than just intelligence dwelt behind his frank, dark eyes," she thought. A sensitive spirit, rare honesty, and a gentleness that must have grown out of his careful Southern upbringing. Brad was a theology and psychology major at Becka's school. He was studying to become a hospital chaplain. His trim, athletic form stood about six inches taller than she. Add to those attributes a handsome, tanned face with a devastating smile, and Becka felt blessed indeed to have Bradley Colton as her boyfriend.

By ten o'clock Becka was able to wear her contact lenses and see clearly all the way to the swimming pool where the rest of her crew was cleaning. She decided to join them.

Tricia called from the smaller wading pool beyond as Becka

walked up. "Hi! Glad to see you're all right!" Tricia stood so short that the trash bag she clung to looked like a tent flapping at her side. "Why don't you help me over here? You can't imagine all the rocks and junk that are cluttering up this place."

Bending over to scoop up more debris, Tricia gasped, then emitted a loud, piercing scream that made Becka stop dead in her tracks.

Chapter 2

Hodgepodgety

"L-l-lizard!" Tricia stammered.

A ghost of a smile nearly betrayed Becka's relief. But then she spotted the half-decayed, bloated body floating at her friend's feet, and her own stomach retched at the sight. "Yuck!" Becka dragged out the word, so it would sound more ladylike. "Andy!" she called. "We need you over here!"

Andy Norris had started in their direction when Tricia screamed. Part Indian, he was deeply tanned, with short, brown hair. Deftly, he seized the offending creature by the tail and hurled it over the fence.

"There, girls!" He grinned as if talking to two silly children. "Is there anything else you need?"

Tricia gave him a wavering look. "Uh—Andy, do you think there are any more creepy-crawly things in here?"

"Might be," he said. "Just call me, though, and I'll charge to your rescue." With that he whirled around and returned to his own task, scrubbing the algae from the Olympic-sized pool.

Becka shook her head. "We'll never be ready in time for those campers when they arrive Sunday."

Tricia was timidly lifting a rock. "I'm afraid you're right," she said, "but we'll do our best today and tomorrow."

Later at lunch Becka complained to Brad, "Honestly, I'm finding it hard to cope with the relaxed way this camp is run. Everything's so disorganized and behind schedule, just the opposite of how Pastor Joe operated Camp Wautum Woods."

Brad set down his juice and regarded Becka with expres-

14

sionless eyes. He didn't say anything.

"What are you thinking?" she asked.

"I'm thinking that there was quite a shake-up in the staff directorship at the last minute, and that probably accounts for our lagging behind schedule." Before Becka could respond, he continued, "And I'm thinking how things are progressing nicely down at the waterfront where I work." He reached across the table and squeezed her hand. "I'm also thinking how much I'd like to take you out for supper this evening. It's our time off, you know."

"I'd like that too!" Becka beamed. "It'll be good to get away from here for awhile, especially from those ants."

"That's right!" Brad said. "Actually, Alec and I got permission to play exterminators this afternoon. Shouldn't take too long to spray those little critters."

After lunch Becka heard the deep voices of Brad and Alec singing from the bridge, "Men in girls' village!" Then, as they hauled an oversized cylinder of spray onto cabin 14's porch, the duet chorused again, "Men entering the cabin!"

While Becka and Tricia directed the guys to the room, Brad said, "Bert the maintenance man guarantees this stuff to work."

"Bert?" Tricia asked. "Isn't his wife the one who's expecting?"

"Any time now," Alec replied. "Brad and I have been arguing over a good name for the baby if it's a boy."

"Yeah!" Brad chuckled. "I suggested the name 'Bradley Alec,' and of course, my friend here likes 'Alec Bradley.' "

With a lame smile, Becka pointed to the baseboard and bunk bed, where the ants scurried along in a churning swirl of red. "Well, there they are!" she said.

"Stand back!" Alec commanded dramatically as he took the hose in his hand and aimed it at the pests. Brad, in turn, pumped the cylinder. A few drops dribbled out.

The girls burst into laughter, while the fellows looked chagrined. All four watched in dismay while the ants side-stepped the poison drops like ladies skirting a puddle at a lawn party.

"You wouldn't happen to have a spray bottle on the premises, would you?" Brad asked.

"Window cleaner," Becka replied, fetching the bottle from the kitchen. She dumped the contents into a bowl, then handed it to her boyfriend. After they filled the container with the poisonous liquid, the young men took turns playing soldier, "zapping" ants left and right.

Meanwhile, the girls' director, Andrea Nolan, dropped by with news about counseling assignments. Andrea's wheat-colored hair formed a single long braid that bobbed behind her as she talked. "Tricia, you'll move into Cabin 14-B here and assist Gwen Pennington."

Becka noted her friend's disappointment, and tried to conceal her own when Andrea told her, "You'll have Eldora Snarr for an assistant counselor in your cabin."

Eldora Snarr! Becka pictured the dark-haired beauty who seemed more interested in makeup and boys than the spiritual aspects of camp.

"Andrea," Becka ventured, "is there any chance that Tricia and I could serve as counselors together instead?"

The girls' director straightened her tall frame and answered firmly, "No chance at all." Then she added, smiling, "We have good reasons for matching you up this way. Consider that, and ask for divine help when you need it."

Becka grumbled silently, "Oh, I'll need it, all right!"

Her drooping spirits rose a little when Brad and Alec emerged triumphantly from her side of the building.

"There you go, girls!" Alec said. "All you have to do is sweep up the little corpses."

"Ew!" Tricia scrunched up her pretty face in disgust. "I've had my fill of corpses for one day."

With the bloated lizard still fresh in her mind, Becka agreed. "So have I. Thanks, guys!"

Brad held the spray cylinder like a knight with a lance primed for battle. "We're off to Cabin 12, where the ants have even invaded their refrigerator."

Alec followed him out, toting the spray bottle. "I'll return this later," he promised.

Tricia looked sober. "I heard that Bert's wife Marlena plans to have her baby right here at El Camino Ranch."

Becka's eyes widened in disbelief. "I can't imagine why she

would want to have the baby in this buggy place!"

"Me neither," Tricia replied. "Maybe it has to do with money." Then she asked, 'Have you seen their little boy Mario?"

Becka grinned. "Yeah. He's a darling."

At two o'clock the girls joined the rest of the staff at the campfire bowl for a skit-planning session.

Becka enjoyed acting. It brought back memories from two summers before when she had smeared herself with brown makeup in order to play Hiawatha's sister during campfires. Then at college she and Bradley had belonged to the same acting group. In fact, that's how they had met. Dreamily, Becka recalled their starring opposite each other in the play, *Our Town*. She, as Emily Webb, draped in an antique wedding gown, had shyly stood at Brad's side as he played the awkward groom, George Gibbs.

Later that day Becka returned to the pool, this time using a weed-trimming machine around the outside of the fence. The trimmer chomped weeds with a vengeance while the counselor eagerly worked up an appetite for her supper date with Brad. But an hour later their plans evaporated when Andrea told the couple they would have to wait until the following afternoon for their jaunt to town.

"I'm sorry," she apologized, "but we're just too far behind schedule and need you here this evening for more planning sessions and practice."

Becka felt like elbowing Brad in the ribs when he had replied with a too cheerful, "Sure thing!"

To make matters worse, cheese garnished every dish on the menu that evening—even the soup—and Becka was allergic to cheese. Knowing it would cause a major stomachache, she decided to forget supper altogether, and slipped quietly back to her empty cabin. Her head throbbed, her body felt weighted down with fatigue, and hunger gnawed at her stomach.

Because Becka didn't cry easily, she surprised herself with a flood of unrestrained tears as she slumped onto her bunk—a touch of homesickness mingled with the disappointment over the canceled dinner date. The week had been a grueling one, what with the obstacle course every morning followed by hours of hard labor. And beneath it all lurked a quiet tension developing between her and Brad. It was something she couldn't identify, but it was there, dark and threatening, just out of reach.

"Maybe it was a mistake coming here this summer." She sniffed, wiping her eyes with a tissue. Then she wondered if, perhaps, she was experiencing a kind of culture shock, similar to what missionaries suffer in foreign fields. She thought again about her mountain home, the tall firs roaring in the wind at night, the rain, the snow, her logger father, her vivacious mother, and Kurt, her younger brother. Then she considered Camp Wautum Woods once more, and how it ran like a well-oiled clock.

"This place is so—so—" She blew her nose. "Hodge-podgety!" That made Becka grin in spite of herself. "It *is* culture shock," she decided.

Slowly, she rose from the bed and repaired her tear-stained face with a cold washcloth, then grabbed her flashlight and hiked back up to the cafeteria.

Eldora moved in with Becka the next afternoon, sporting "tons" of luggage and camping gear. A cloud of long, dark hair floated about her head as the assistant arranged her belongings in her part of the cabin, actually a second room. Despite an air of indifference, the anxiety in Eldora's brown eyes divulged the uneasiness she felt about her new role. Becka tried to put the girl at ease by chattering about her early days as an assistant counselor. Before long both of them were laughing like old friends.

A little later Becka and Brad took flight in his polished Mustang toward the nearby city. When they drove through the Pecan Grove, Becka asked about the group of tents she noticed pitched among trees. He explained that they belonged to academy students training for a mission trip to Mexico.

The city streets were clogged with rush-hour, stop-and-go traffic. But eventually they reached a store that sold wet suits. Becka was considering buying one for Brad's upcoming birthday. With the threat of thick traffic, they left early in order to get back to El Camino Ranch in time for vespers.

"Don't worry!" Brad consoled her. "Tomorrow evening everyone has time off. We'll get that supper I promised."

Becka stretched lazily beside him. "I'll look forward to it," she said.

When dusk dimmed the day, Becka found herself next to Tricia and other staff members huddled beside the still, muddy waters of The Pond. Sabbath began with the setting sun, and the campers stood reverently, listening to a sermon—and stood, and stood, and stood.

Finally, after blackness had settled around them, Becka and Tricia cautiously stepped into the water for the footwashing service before communion. Recalling the dead lizard again and wondering about the other slimy creatures that might be bedding down in The Pond, Becka nervously bit her lip as she felt the deep mud ooze through her trembling toes. "Please, don't scream like you did yesterday!" she warned Tricia.

The other girl muffled a squeal. "Oh, Becka! Let's hurry this up before—"

"Don't say it!" Becka cut in. "My imagination's working just fine—too fine!"

Quickly, they took turns splashing water on each other's feet, then climbed onto the dirt bank where they prayed for each other.

Tricia hugged her. "Thanks, friend!"

Becka could sense the girl's twisted smile as they both slipped their muddy feet back into their shoes.

"So much for clean sneakers!" Becka breathed.

After the communion service, the camp director handed out candles. In no time the candles were glowing like miniature spotlights, inviting every flying insect in the Southwest to their service, or so it seemed.

Mosquitoes, moths, and other strange, winged bugs zoomed into the candlelight, feasting on the arms and legs that stood rigidly at attention.

When a time of testimonies followed, Becka's back began to ache as she wriggled, and swatted mosquitoes. What should have been a beautiful spiritual time turned into torture.

On and on staff members talked, sharing answered prayers and praises to God. Finally, with the gritty mud caked inside her shoes, Becka hobbled back to her cabin, where she slept like a dead woman.

The next morning she awakened refreshed and eager for the Waldensian Walk after breakfast. Mack Nolan, the boys' director and Andrea's husband, told the story of Peter Waldo, one of the original Waldenses. These were Christians who, because of persecution, had scattered, some even going to the wilderness. Mack explained how every Sabbath morning the campers would hear this story, then divide into groups. Each person in a group would need to carry a concealed—or memorized—Bible verse throughout their journey and be able to read or recite it at the end. Each group would have a leader—plus a "deceiver" who would try to lead the group astray. "Persecutors" would interrupt their journey and search the campers for their Bible verses, confiscating as many as they could find.

Becka and Brad were happily part of the same group. She memorized her verse, Psalm 50:15: "Call upon me in the day of trouble: I will deliver thee, and thou shalt glorify me." Then they began the long, rugged walk that stretched over each new horizon. Mile after mile they followed the pre-marked course. At first Becka enjoyed the journey, the arid beauty of the countryside, until the brambles grew thick and the sun beat down on them with a torturous heat, causing two girls in another group to faint.

When they finally returned to the cafeteria, Mack looked sheepish. "Uh—I think we'll shorten the Waldensian Walk a bit," he said.

Groans sounded throughout the large hall.

He corrected himself. "We'll shorten it a lot."

Instantly, the groans turned to cheers.

With practicing scenes for the Walk Through the Bible, the rest of Sabbath passed swiftly.

Then in the evening Becka and Brad swooped down from the hills in his air-conditioned car toward an Italian restaurant where they ate spaghetti by candlelight.

Becka giggled. "What a difference between this candlelight and last night's bug invasion!"

"Oh, I don't know," Brad replied defensively. "I rather enjoyed last evening's service."

Becka looked incredulous. "You did?"

He smiled. "Yes, I really did. I mean, it was a little long, but, you know . . ."

"Long!" Becka's voice trembled with emotion. "*Everything* is long at El Camino Ranch. The obstacle course is long, the sermons are long, the Waldensian Walk was unending."

"Becka!" Brad pleaded.

"Yes?"

His face looked grimly composed. "We'd better get back to camp."

"No time to linger?" she asked.

"No," he answered bluntly.

Becka could feel that quiet tension again, looming larger than ever. "At Camp Wautum Woods we got an entire twenty-four-hour day off," she protested. "Here they only give us a few hours."

"I know," Brad replied as he opened the car door for her.

They traveled back to the ranch in silence. She couldn't stand the tension one moment more and blurted, "Brad, please tell me what's been bothering you."

He braked the car in front of her cabin. "You want the truth?"

Becka turned and faced him squarely as if to a firing squad. "The whole truth."

He eyed her with an appraising look. "OK," he began, "you were one of those privileged kids who got to attend Christian schools all your life. I didn't. You got a good dose of religion every day. Except for Mom and Dad, I didn't."

She frowned, wondering, "What does my attending Christian schools have to do with Brad?"

"My greatest exposure to religion—when Jesus became real to me—was here at El Camino Ranch every summer."

"It was?" Becka stiffened, suddenly feeling like a spoiled child.

"In fact," Brad said, "it was at this very camp that I gave my life to the Lord last summer and was baptized in that swimming pool you've been cleaning all week."

Shame washed through her. "Oh," she said, wishing she could take back all the insults she had hurled at El Camino

Ranch throughout the week.

"This ranch is very meaningful to me," he continued. "Those counselors loved me and showed me Jesus. I want to do the same now for other campers." He exhaled with obvious impatience. "Becka, every time you compare El Camino Ranch to Camp Wautum Woods or tell me how unorganized we are, or whatever, it's as if you're insulting a good friend of mine, and it hurts me deeply."

"Oh, Brad!" she exclaimed. "I'm so sorry. Please, forgive me!" Becka threw her arms around his neck. "I wouldn't hurt you deliberately for any amount of money," she said. "I'm just a little homesick and may be suffering some culture shock in this place."

She leaned back in the bucket seat and was relieved to see compassion in her boyfriend's face. "I'll try to look for the positive things here instead," she promised. "And I have to admit, this *is* a beautiful camp."

A few moments later, watching Brad drive away, Becka gazed up at the star-studded sky and wondered, "Is Brad's and my friendship strong enough to survive this summer?"

She knew only time held the answer to that question.

Chapter 3
Tammy and Terry

Andrea's announcement surprised Becka: "Three of the high school girls who were going to Mexico to help build a church have decided to stay here and help us instead." Then the girls' director dispatched orders. "Becka and Eldora will take Tammy; Gwen and Tricia will have Terry; and Carmen will help in Cabin 12."

Questions tumbled around in Becka's head. Then she voiced one of them aloud: "Why would these girls miss a trip to Mexico?"

Tricia made a humming noise in her throat. "Boys, maybe?"

"I hope not."

Eight adventure campers filled Becka's cabin, along with her two assistants, Eldora and Tammy. Becka loved the general hubbub of getting acquainted while the girls unpacked and set up housekeeping, and she especially loved this age group. At eight and nine years, most of her campers glowed with expectancy, ready to soak up all the delights offered at El Camino Ranch.

There was Heide, a hyperactive-but-fun string bean of a girl with dark hair. Chubby Holly already missed her family and was fluttering in and out of the first stages of homesickness. Heather, a cowgirl type, had blond hair and a constant smile. And Jackie, with her willing-to-help-anyone attitude, could have been voted Miss Congeniality for the week.

Becka learned at the onset that tall, dark Elsa would be their lagger. "There's always one tortoise in every group," she

23

complained to Eldora. The two counselors took turns dragging Elsa up hills.

It soon became obvious that Elsa desperately longed for acceptance from the other girls. That was where Lela, the "manipulator," stepped in. When Becka asked Lela to pick up her several pairs of shoes strewn throughout the cabin, the counselor overhead an interesting conversation.

"Elsa," Lela cooed, "I'll become your best friend if you'll pick up my shoes for me."

Becka's face flared when she peeked around the corner and spotted the tall, dark girl arranging sneakers under the bunk while Lela sat above her like a queen on a throne, gloating over her newfound servant.

The counselor held her tongue, though, and waited until worship time that night to illustrate a lesson for "the queen." Becka told the story of Peter denying Christ three times before the rooster crowed.

"Then Jesus gave Peter a very loving, sad look," she said. "That made Peter feel so bad, he went out and wept and asked God to forgive him." She paused for effect, then looked directly at Lela. "Jesus was a real friend. Real friends don't ask people to do things for them just to *use* them."

A light glinted in Lela's eyes. Then she glared at Becka.

Ouch! That one backfired. But the counselor took comfort in an earlier triumph. After the nightly service Lela had led two other cabinmates ahead of their group, directly against orders. Instead of scolding them, Becka took off running, passed them, and called back, "You want to run? Let's go!"

Away she flew, with three breathless campers on her heels. "Wait! Don't go so fast!" they begged.

Becka congratulated herself on the simple solution. She decided that anytime her little rebels wanted to run ahead, she would join them and challenge them to a race.

On Monday afternoon Becka noticed something about Tammy, her newest assistant, that disturbed her. Tawny and talkative, the girl was constantly babbling about her many boyfriends, prompting the young campers to socialize with certain fellows at the ranch.

As soon as Becka found a free moment, she ushered the

high school girl into the kitchen where she could chat with her privately. "Tammy," she began in her gentlest voice, "I realize this is your first experience with counseling, but there are a couple of things you need to know." Becka sent up a quick, silent prayer, then plunged ahead. "I expect to encounter boy-crazy girls in junior and especially teen camps, but not in this one. Adventure campers aren't to that stage yet. Please don't encourage it."

Tammy pouted. "I was only trying to be friendly."

"Good!" Becka gave her a warm smile. "But be friendly in other ways. Remember, we're supposed to be drawing these girls to Jesus, not filling their heads with distractions."

Tammy grunted, then stalked back to the room, leaving Becka to wonder about her choice of words.

After Becka finished teaching beginners at the pool all afternoon, she waited for Brad to return from the waterfront for their daily two-hour break.

"Want to go to town?" he asked.

"Oh, I don't know," Becka answered. "Why don't we eat at the cafeteria? Tonight's the greased watermelon race at the pool, and I'd love to watch the kids."

So they ate together in the lodge, taking care to act platonic. No handholding allowed in front of the campers!

Becka glowed when she talked about her girls. "Most of them are absolute darlings," she told him. "So innocent!"

"I've got a good group of boys too," Brad echoed her sentiments. "There's one little guy, though, who loves his shirt."

"His shirt?"

"Yes, a blue-and-white one with dolphins swimming all over it. The kid has worn the same shirt for two days. He refuses to change it."

Becka laughed. "Those dolphins will look awfully dirty by tomorrow."

"They already are." Brad grinned. "Sounds like the name of a football team or something—the Dirty Dolphins!"

After the greased watermelon race and free swim, Becka returned with her girls to their cabin for cleanup before campfire. When she asked them to hang up their wet bathing suits, everyone did—except Lela. She defied the counselor, flashing her an unspoken, "Make me!"

Too tired to confront the girl, Becka chose to ignore her instead. At the same time she noticed that Tammy wasn't improving. Not only was the helper still dwelling on guys she had dated, now she was adding modern music to her conversations with the youngsters.

"Maybe our talk will eventually soak in," Becka hoped.

That evening Becka took turns with Eldora again, pulling Elsa up the hill to The Rim for campfire. Exhausted, Becka sat down heavily, then grinned at Brad, who was perched beside the little boy in the blue-and-white dolphin shirt."

Becka read her boyfriend's lips: "The shirt goes tomorrow!"

"We'll see," she mused.

The next morning at line call Becka noticed a proud Bradley Colton. His camper had changed the shirt—finally. But the dolphins were back at lunch, and Brad looked exasperated.

"By Sunday that shirt will be able to walk out of here on its own!" Becka thought. She wished her problems were that simple. Tension was mounting between herself and Tammy. She suspected the girl of using her expensive hair conditioner and of wolfing down the granola bars Becka kept in the refrigerator. *If she would only ask* . . . But that wasn't the worst of it. Several clues hinted that both high school girls, Tammy and Terry, might be sneaking out at night. Two of her young campers had reported that tapping on the window had awakened them. And the next morning Tammy and Terry looked unusually tired.

Becka didn't voice her suspicions to the girls' director until Thursday, when Tricia complained about Terry's crankiness. "It's as if she's not getting much sleep."

"Well, I'll just stay up later tonight," Andrea promised, "and conduct some extra room checks."

After the talent show and campfire Thursday evening, Becka's girls trooped back to their cabin to prepare for bed and worship time. In their weariness, her campers eagerly retired after that.

Becka tried to stay awake for when Andrea came by for room check at eleven, but she, too, drifted off. The next thing she realized, Tricia was tugging at her and whispering frantically, "Wake up! There are some prowlers outside my window!"

Becka awoke in an instant. She grabbed her robe and tiptoed over to Eldora's bunk, waking her. The three met Tricia's assistant, Gwen, in the kitchen.

"I'm scared," Gwen admitted. "A couple of guys were hanging around outside my cabin."

Becka's heart pounded like a muffled drum. There wasn't any phone to call for help, and she knew none of them was brave enough to venture out into the darkness. *The door was unlocked!*

Barely breathing, they listened to the night sounds: their campers snoozing, the crickets chirping throughout the hills . . .

Then it came to her, "Tammy and Terry! Are they in their bunks?"

"Yes," Tricia responded. "I don't think they're asleep, but they are in their bedrolls."

Just then a flashlight beamed on the front porch and sent chills prickling along Becka's spine. The four girls exhaled in unison when they realized it was Andrea.

Hastily, they related the news.

"Mmmm!" Andrea replied, deep in thought. "There must be some boys unaccounted for, roaming around out here—in girls' village, of all things! I'd love to catch them." Her grin looked wicked in the flashlight's glow. "I'll stay up extra late and do room checks every half-hour," she whispered, then added, "Incidentally, Building 12's counselors suspect Carmen of sneaking out also. Now you girls get some sleep!"

Reluctantly, Becka returned to bed, but how could she sleep with her heart still racing at top speed? "Andrea's so brave," she thought. "She has a lot more faith than I do, wandering around out there in the night." She listened to her clock ticking endlessly in her ear.

At 2:30 a.m. Becka heard a strange sound and leapt from her bed, running for the lobby, where she collided with Tricia in the dark. Both girls gasped with fright.

"What are you trying to do?" Becka whispered. "Give me a heart attack?"

"Me?" Tricia sounded wounded. She clung to Becka's arm while they peeked out the screen door at the moonlit hills.

"Do you see anything?" Becka asked.

"No."

Suddenly, both girls were aware of another presence in the room with them. There, sprawled on a mattress at their feet lay Tricia's helper, Terry, pretending to be fast asleep. The moonlight reflected off her full set of clothes—even shoes!

Tricia's eyes gleamed mischievously in the dimness. "Becka," she asked aloud, "what's Terry doing, lying here in her regular clothes?"

"I haven't the foggiest notion, Tricia. What do you think?"

"I think she wants to sneak out, but the girls' director keeps coming by, so she can't."

"Yeah," Becka agreed dramatically. "It does look mighty suspicious. I believe we'd better tell Andrea when she comes back." She paused. "Terry?"

"Yes?" came the quick reply.

"You're supposed to be in bed."

"OK," she snapped, then made a beeline for her room.

The two counselors covered their mouths to suppress their laughter. After all, poor Terry had suffered enough. They couldn't humiliate her further.

Next, the girls found a couple of boxes to set in the cabin doorways, so if anyone tried to escape they would make a noise and awaken the counselors.

A few hours later Becka groaned at her bloodshot eyes in the mirror. "How have those high school girls gone without so much sleep this week?" she wondered. "I can't even skip one night without feeling—and looking—terrible."

But Terry and Tammy did look equally haggard that morning, and walked silently through the day as if a gloomy stormcloud hung over them.

Becka looked forward to Elder Jackson's morning sermon. She knew it would help revive her. Elder Jackson was a true Cajun, straight from the swamplands of Louisiana. He selected a word each morning for the campers to listen for, and every time he uttered that word they were to shout, "Amen!" It was great fun and kept the campers and staff on their toes.

At Friday night vespers Elder Jackson outdid himself. First, he began his sermon with a huge boat-shaped bowl and some bananas. He peeled the fruit and sliced them down the center, arranging them neatly in the dish. "These bananas represent *patience*," he told them.

Next, he brought out several cartons of ice cream and scooped up mounds of chocolate, vanilla, and strawberry to cover the bananas. "The ice cream is *respect*."

Amused, Becka watched the youngsters ogling the treat before them. Elder Jackson was holding a jar of chopped walnuts and sprinkled them generously over the top. "These nuts represent *sharing*." Then he took out a can of whipped cream and squirted it all over the giant banana split. "This is for *helping*." Next, most of a jar of cherries sunk into the whipped cream. "The cherries are a symbol of *love*," he said. Then he looked out in the audience and asked, "Would some of you like to sample this banana split for me?"

Hands flew up all over the place as he handed out plastic spoons. Becka gleefully caught a glimpse of Brad, but he wasn't smiling. In fact, his mouth looked tightly drawn. She wished she could leave her girls and go ask him what was troubling him.

After everyone had settled back down, Elder Jackson took out a can of motor oil labeled *jealousy* and said, "It took all that time to build this yummy banana split which represents *friendship*, but it takes only a second or two to destroy it." With that, he poured motor oil all over the ice cream goodies, bringing loud groans of protest from the campers.

The illustration was a powerful one that Becka was still pondering long after her girls were in bed. She was thinking about her special friendship with Brad and about the tense look on his face during the sermon that evening. She hoped she hadn't said or done anything again to offend him.

Becka was still awake when Andrea dropped by for room check. The girls' director looked worn out. Tricia joined them.

"Counselors," Andrea began, "I must tell you that your helpers, Tammy and Terry, came to me in tears today, complaining about how you've been treating them."

Becka looked astonished. "*We've* been treating *them*?"

"Don't worry! I really leveled with them about their irresponsible behavior. We had quite a session." Andrea heaved a giant sigh. "They said they felt so discouraged that they've decided not to return to El Camino Ranch for teen camp."

Remorse swept through Becka. "You know," she admitted, "I think Tammy and I could have become pretty good friends if we hadn't started out on the wrong foot."

"Yes," Tricia agreed. "And I feel sorry for them. After all, they gave up their trip to Mexico for . . . for . . ."

"A week of irresponsible behavior, for the most part," Andrea repeated. "It's sad really. Anyway, would you do your best to make their final Sabbath here an enjoyable one?"

"Of course!" Becka replied as she glanced out the window. "Hey! That looks like your husband, Andrea." Then Becka squinted at the silhouette beside Mack. "And that looks like Brad beside him."

"Oh, that's the next item I was supposed to share with you," Andrea said. "Mack's taking your boyfriend to the hospital emergency room."

"What?" Becka felt stunned as she rushed out onto the porch and watched the car disappear down the winding road.

Chapter 4

Trouble With Eldora

Becka slept lightly, waking often, wondering about Brad. According to Andrea, his back was in excruciating pain. "Probably too many hours on water skis," the girls' director had suggested before leaving Becka alone with her anxiety.

Becka rushed to staff worship the next morning and greeted Brad cheerfully when he arrived.

"The doctor said my back muscles were really tight, and that was causing the problem," he explained. "So he gave me a shot of muscle relaxant, and I'm feeling lots better this morning."

Becka studied the gray pallor on his face. "Good enough for the Waldensian Walk?" she asked.

"Not quite."

Relief flooded over her when she noted the familiar sparkle returning to his eyes. "I have to suffer during that time," he teased. "I'll be exiled to the air-conditioned staff lounge." Then he added with feigned sincerity, "Of course, I'll be thinking about you out there on those hot hills, leading your pilgrims."

"Of course!" Becka was thoughtful a moment. "You know, if the Deceiver in my group is extra good and I hang back a little, maybe he can lead all my kids astray. Then I'd be free to return to camp and could visit with you in the lounge."

"Great idea! I hope you can."

Later at line call Becka saw Brad again, still looking pale, but at his post, shepherding his boys into formation.

"Oh, I hope the Deceiver steals my entire group from me,"

she thought. After all, she deserved a rest after several nights of little sleep.

Two earnest young fellows, however, had taken Mack's warning to heart. Almost immediately the Deceiver led all the others in Becka's group onto the wrong path, but not those two determined boys. They stuck to Becka's trail like fly paper. None of her diversionary tactics worked. She led the lone pair through all three miles of the journey to the end—Bible verses intact.

Despite her disappointment, Becka had to admire those short, sandy-haired survivors. She heaped praises upon them like confetti while they squirmed shyly, nudging each other.

"You know, boys," she began, "in a few years you'll feel a lot of pressure to follow the group, to do whatever they're doing even when it's wrong." She eyed them soberly. "I hope, when that time comes, you'll remember today and how you stuck to the *right* trail even when all the other kids took another path. I hope you'll never be afraid to be different—when it's the right thing to do."

They grinned proudly, then raced away when she finally climbed off her imaginary soap box and dismissed them.

After lunch and rest period, Becka led her campers to the cafeteria for Sabbath School and church services. Late afternoon brought the long-awaited Walk Through the Bible. This summer the walk featured various scenes from the life of the apostle Peter.

After Becka's scene was finished, she followed the campers around The Pond to where Brad and Alec performed the notorious walking-on-the-water episode. Brad had shared his fears earlier about the rickety, submerged dock they would tread upon to simulate the miracle, but the hidden dock stood firm and so did the performance.

The last scene was of Peter's upside-down crucifixion. Scott Meadows portrayed the aging Peter in this act. Scott and his bride, Kay, had come to work at the ranch just hours after their wedding.

"What a way to spend your honeymoon!" Becka thought. She held her breath as Scott raced through his lines hanging upside down, his face turning a deep shade of red. Then his eyes began to bulge, as if his head would explode any moment.

Hastily, the guides herded the campers away so Joel could help Scott off the cross. Becka sighed with relief when the newlywed's face returned to its natural color.

"How dreadful that must have been for the real Peter!" she imagined, realizing the apostle hadn't felt worthy to be cruci-fied in the same manner as Jesus.

After the awards ceremony the next morning Becka watched Tammy, her volunteer, mope about the cabin, packing.

"Tammy, I really did appreciate the extra help," she said.

"Yeah?"

"Yeah." Becka put on her warmest smile. "I just wish things had worked out better for you."

"Thanks!" came the girl's clipped reply.

Soon Becka and other counselors were swarmed with de-parting campers, all hugging and calling goodbyes. Even Lela, the "manipulator," looked grateful for her stay at El Camino Ranch.

"Well, one week down," Becka muttered to herself, wonder-ing what her next group would bring.

She met all nine of them when Eldora brought the girls to free swim at the pool where Becka was on duty. There was one blonde in the group of dark-haired juniors. Becka liked the fair Beth at once. The girl's soft features matched her soft voice and smile. Becka noticed that the two sisters, Fawn and Fern, appeared standoffish, huddling together in a corner of the pool. She thought Fawn looked too mature for junior camp, and so did Carol and Cheryl.

"Fawn's fifteen," Eldora told her, "but she wanted to be with her ten-year-old sister."

"What about the two short ones?" Becka asked.

"Carol and Cheryl are thirteen," Eldora replied. "So is Marelda." Already this well-tanned teenager cocked her head in such a way as to say to the world, "I'm better than you are."

Annette looked as if she were cut from the same mold, with her pouty lips and upturned nose.

But petite Tonya, a Mexican-American girl, gave Becka courage. Tonya, with her long, dark ponytail, provided sweet company that afternoon. And tall, thin Katrina also proved to be nice.

Becka scolded herself for prejudging the group. "Maybe Marelda and Annette are just covering up shyness," she hoped.

The next morning everyone was tired and dragging behind schedule. "Girls, if we don't get up to line call on time, they'll make us stay after and humiliate us."

"Ew!" exclaimed Marelda. "I can't stand being humiliated."

"Then let's hurry!" Becka coaxed them all through the lobby, out the door, and up the hill.

The hot morning air slapped at her face. "How can it be so hot already?" she wondered. "Hurry!" she called. All nine of her girls, along with the two counselors, scrambled quickly up to the lodge just in time.

"Whew!" Becka breathed as she watched the flagraising ceremony. Suddenly, she felt someone nudge her.

"Becka," Katrina whispered. "I don't feel good."

The counselor studied the girl a few moments. She did look a little red in the face. "You're just hungry, Honey. We'll have breakfast in a few minutes. Then you'll be just fine. Now, go get back in line."

"OK," Katrina said as she whirled around. Without warning, she staggered forward. Becka and Eldora gasped, reaching for the girl—but not in time to keep her from toppling face first onto the pavement.

Brad came out of nowhere and scooped up the unconscious camper. "I'll take her to the nurse's station," he offered.

Stunned, Becka grunted something. "If she had just said, 'I feel dizzy,' I would have had a clue she was about to faint. How stupid of me!"

Anxiously, she waited for Brad's return to the cafeteria, where the lodge clanked and hummed with dining noises. "The nurse diagnosed it as heat exhaustion," he reported.

"Heat exhaustion at 7:30 in the morning?" Becka looked shocked.

"That's right," Brad said. "It's nearly 90 degrees already. Besides, she probably hasn't drunk much water since she's been here. Add a run up the hill to that, and you get heat exhaustion. She'll be OK in a little while."

When the nurse brought Katrina into the cafeteria later,

the bruised girl became the instant envy of the cabin.

"Oh, Katrina!" Cheryl trilled breathlessly. "Handsome Brad Colton picked you up in his strong arms." Amid squeals from some of the other girls, she added, "How lucky can you get?"

Becka smiled smugly to herself.

That afternoon a familiar form limped over to the swimming pool.

"Brad!" Becka exclaimed. "What did you do to yourself now?"

"I twisted my leg. Nurse said I can teach swimming instead, but no skiing for a few days."

"I'm sorry," she lied. She and Brad would be working side by side!

He lowered his muscular frame into the pool and began to encourage one young fellow named Rodney. "He's a rascal," Brad whispered to Becka, "a real prankster in our cabin. But I like the kid. Hey, Rodney!" he called, "want to learn to dive?"

"Sure!" the freckle-faced youngster shouted back and dog-paddled over to the counselor.

Becka grimaced as Rodney belly-flopped again and again, making giant splashes in the pool.

"Told you the kid's OK," Brad chuckled. "He won't quit till he gets it right." And Rodney did—finally.

The playful, gentle way Brad instructed the boys touched a wellspring of emotion in Becka. "Not too many guys take such a genuine interest in these kids," she thought.

The next few days Becka looked forward to her job at the pool like a four-year-old looks forward to Christmas. And Brad was Santa Claus, making the mornings and afternoons fun-filled. Still, they both had to guard their feelings and act overly businesslike in front of the children.

Wednesday at supper Eldora reported that Fawn's sister Fern had fallen off a horse and been taken to the hospital. Becka suggested that their group pray for the girl.

The lone sister ate silently, apparently lost in her private worry.

Becka had noticed an undercurrent buzzing through her cabin. Something was happening between the two sisters and Carol and Cheryl—muffled words, sharp glances—though nothing Becka could pinpoint. But she suspected a volcano of some sort, ready to erupt.

Also, Eldora's behavior was grating on Becka's nerves. The assistant, who was in charge of four of the girls in her end of the cabin, wasn't keeping her room in order. Then Wednesday night Eldora allowed her girls to talk and giggle long after lights were out.

Waiting for Fern to return from the hospital, Becka marched into Eldora's room. "Uh, lights went out a half-hour ago."

"Oh, that's all right!" Eldora sang. "I told the girls they could talk."

"But they're disturbing the other campers who need their sleep," Becka countered. As everyone grew quiet, she could easily guess their thoughts: *What's this? A disagreement between the counselors?*

"But I was just telling them about one of my old boyfriends, and we were sharing stories . . ."

"Eldora," Becka began, choosing her words carefully, "as head counselor, I insist that everyone quiet down. There'll be plenty of time to talk tomorrow." Becka padded back to her bunk, and in minutes all the campers were sound asleep.

But not Becka. It seemed that Tammy's worldly spirit had stayed behind with Eldora. Now Eldora was talking boys, makeup, and modern music with her girls—anything to snuff out the spiritual benefits of camp life. "I must talk to Andrea about her," she decided.

Just as Becka drifted off, she was awakened by the girls' director, who had brought Fern back. "No broken bones," she reported. "She's just limping and can't ride horses for the rest of the week. She'll be OK."

Becka smiled sleepily. "I'm so glad. That's an answer to our prayers."

The next morning she sought out Andrea in the cafeteria and told her about the problem with Eldora.

"I'm sorry, Becka, but I don't have time to talk to her right now," Andrea said. "Why don't you try first? If that doesn't work, I'll counsel with her."

With the recent encounter with Tammy looming large in

her mind, Becka agreed reluctantly. That afternoon during quiet time she asked her assistant to join her in the kitchen. "*Deja vu,*" she thought.

"Eldora," she began. "I like you. You're fun to work with, but this week we've been experiencing some trouble."

"Yeah, I know," her assistant replied. "It's because you're a lot more strict than I am."

Becka took a deep breath. "I don't think it's a matter of leniency versus strictness. I think it's a matter of acting like a friend first, counselor second."

Eldora looked ready to duel. "What's wrong with being their friend?"

"Well, you lose the control a counselor should have." Becka talked very carefully, with deep thought between sentences. "I feel there's a lack of the spiritual atmosphere we should have in our cabin."

"Our worship times are OK," Eldora said.

"Yes, but that's only a small portion of the day," Becka replied. She talked on, pointing out the need for more discipline when it came to cabin neatness and inspections.

But Eldora wouldn't relinquish her stand. "Well, I think I'm doing a great job as an assistant counselor," she huffed.

Just then a loud voice screeched from their cabin, "Stop treating me like dirt!" Crashing sounds followed.

A fresh wave of anxiety gripped Becka, blotting out the dispute with her assistant. Both counselors charged for the door and flung it open in time to see Fawn, with angry tears streaming down her face, stamping around the room and throwing things—hard things!

She screamed again, "Don't tell me what to do!"

Chapter 5

Fire!

Becka grabbed Fawn's arm just as it was about to swing at the frightened-looking Carol. Cheryl, equally scared, cowered behind her friend.

Twisting in the counselor's grip, Fawn blustered, "Let me at 'em!" A flurry of hot accusations came spitting out, then in a smaller, trembling voice, she choked, "Those two've been insulting my sis and me all week."

Becka's grip held firm as she guided the girl over to her bunk. Eldora, in turn, steered Carol and Cheryl into the other room.

"Now," said Becka, "tell me what this is about." The rest of the girls, their ears stretching to catch every word, pretended to sleep.

Still seething with rage, Fawn's eyes narrowed. "Ever since we got here Carol and Cheryl have been mean to my little sister and me."

"How?" Becka asked.

Fawn pretended to take on Carol's prissy voice, seesawing her head back and forth. " 'Fawn, you'd better clean up your bed now,' she'd whisper. 'Fawn, you'd better do this, you'd better do that.' Cheryl too—all week long. They made me feel like my sis and I were trash. I just couldn't stand it anymore." Then the dark girl thrust her hands to her face and wept as if her heart would break. "They're younger than I am," she sobbed. "They had no right to boss me like that."

Becka agreed soothingly and wrapped her arms around the

girl, letting her cry freely on her shoulder. She could hear Eldora's firm voice in the next room, lecturing the pair in question about their "bigotry" and "unchristian behavior."

"Mmmm!" Becka pondered. "Maybe there's some depth to my assistant after all!" Handing Fawn a tissue, the counselor asked, "Do you feel better now?"

"A little."

Becka's eyes focused on the tearstained face. "It wasn't right for those girls to treat you like that," she said. "But losing your temper in such a harsh way wasn't right either. If you had come to me about it, Honey, I could have taken care of the situation a long time ago. Then none of this would have happened."

"I suppose. It's just that—that I've always stuck up for Fern, ya know."

Becka half smiled and brushed some stray hair from the girl's forehead. "Why don't we pray and ask the Lord to help you feel good feelings toward Carol and Cheryl?"

Fawn stiffened, frowning. "I don't know. They've been pretty mean to us."

Becka talked some more to the girl, then prayed with her. When she had finished, Eldora brought Carol and Cheryl in.

They sheepishly said "I'm sorry" to Fawn and Fern, and the two sisters grunted some weak apologies in return. This time there was no tirade of angry words. Just a calm awkwardness and even hints of a penitent spirit on both sides.

Becka sighed inwardly, feeling she had just scored another small victory. But with dread she wondered if the battle between her and Eldora would continue all summer.

Thursday Becka and Brad returned to the sports shop during their time off. Again he combed through the rack of multicolored wet suits, finally deciding upon a charcoal-gray outfit with a fluorescent pink strip running full length down its side.

While he modeled the suit, Becka wrinkled up her face with indecision. "I'm not sure," she reflected aloud, noting the way the tank top enhanced his muscular chest.

"Doesn't it look good?" Brad asked.

"That's just it!" she laughed. "It looks *too* good. Already half the girls at El Camino Ranch have a crush on you. Now I'll be competing with *all* of them!"

His mouth opened speechlessly, then he grinned. Glancing at a nearby saleslady, he lowered his voice and said with the sincerity of a smitten poet, "No one can compete with you, beautiful lady!" Then he escaped to the dressing room, leaving Becka's blush of pleasure undetected.

A few minutes later she purchased the wet suit with the money she had saved for Brad's present, all the while complaining about his seeing it before his birthday.

They strolled hand-in-hand across the parking lot. "Considering the brief moments we have together," he said, "it was the practical way to do it—and very thoughtful of you," he added.

"Yeah, I know," she agreed pompously. Her heart swelled when she realized how pleased Brad looked about his gift.

The rest of the day and Friday ran smoothly until Eldora left for her time off with her visiting boyfriend, Marty.

"Did you see his sports car?" raved Annette, amidst giggles. "What a dream!"

After supper Becka struggled to get both rooms ready for inspection. "Girls," she pleaded, "Mack will be here before Sabbath begins. He'll take off points for the tiniest smudge on a mirror or window. Come on!" she exclaimed like a cheerleader whose squad had deserted her. "Let's make this place sparkle!"

Her campers responded without enthusiasm. But it was Friday, and everyone was tired, including Becka herself. No matter how she prodded them, the girls seemed to move in slow motion. Suddenly one of the campers squealed, "Eldora and Marty are back!" Instantly, the window was crammed with campers as they watched the couple in the red sports car. The campers had discovered some latent energy.

Not wishing to sound like a jealous stepsister, Becka gently coaxed them back to their tasks. "Surely, Eldora will say goodbye and come in and help," she thought.

But Eldora didn't come in—even when Mack arrived for inspection. The campers, lined up in formation on the porch, gaped at the couple still talking in the car while Mack stepped inside the building with his checklist.

Becka then hustled her group up the hill to the cafeteria for campfire vespers. "Guys are allowed to drop off their dates in girls' village," she thought in exasperation, "but they're not supposed to linger."

Some time later she noticed the couple slipping into the back of the lodge. Becka could feel the ire building in her. "I'd really like to tell that girl a thing or two," she fumed silently. "Her time off ended long ago." She took a couple of deep breaths to cool down.

In spite of the earlier trouble, Becka's cabin still received good marks for inspection. That helped soothe her ruffled feelings, and she decided to say little to Eldora about the incident.

The next morning during the Waldensian Walk, Becka noticed how dry the countryside looked. No early morning dew clung to the bleached grass now. The heat seemed to penetrate to her bones, and she longed for the air-conditioning in the cafeteria. Because her group finished the walk early, they all stood restlessly on the hot blacktop, shifting from one frying sneaker to another. No one was allowed inside until all the groups had returned for line call.

"We'll roast to death before everyone gets here," she fretted, wiping her brow.

Just then she saw a familiar car. Brad's parents were pulling into the parking lot. She had nearly forgotten that they were coming for Sabbath School and church, and that they planned to take Brad and her to town that evening after sunset to celebrate their son's birthday. The sight of Brad, dressed in his Sabbath suit, sprinting up the hillside, made Becka's heart quicken. He raced over to open the door for his mother. Becka watched him help her out of the car and gently place a kiss on her forehead.

A woman of extraordinary femininity, Mrs. Colton looked striking in the tan print dress she wore. Even the grueling years, raising three children while working as a full-time secretary, had failed to erase the beauty she had possessed when Brad's father proposed to her nearly thirty years before.

Just as the woman returned her son's hug, a boy raced up the hill, screaming, "Fire! Fire!"

Without a moment's hesitation Brad and his father scrambled down the hill toward boys' village, where Becka spotted a thin veil of smoke rising from the direction of Alec's cabin. Herb Wheatley, the fireman, fled for the pumper truck with others hot on his heels.

The color had drained from Tricia's face. "Oh! I hope Alec and his boys are all right!" she breathed.

Mrs. Colton rushed over to the girls, briefly surveyed the growing cloud of smoke to the west, and visibly gathered her wits. "I'm sure they'll be fine," she told the girls. Then she cast a wavering look at Becka. "I wish I could say the same for Brad's and my husband's good suits and shoes!"

Becka smiled weakly. "Welcome to El Camino Ranch!" She felt helplessly marooned on the hill, watching the smoke billow now above the trees while Tricia paced restlessly at the parking lot's edge.

Tricia was in noticeable agony. "Surely, it would be OK for us to run down to boys' village in an emergency like this!" she speculated.

"I wouldn't try it," Becka replied, putting her arm around the distraught girl. A bird crooned in a nearby cedar, and aromas drifted over from the kitchen as if all were well and no fire threatened to engulf the entire camp.

Soon they noticed that the smoke was growing thinner. Then it disappeared almost as suddenly as it had begun.

At long last the counselors returned, looking sooty and disheveled, but it took some time to sort themselves out before the camp director could prompt line call into order. "The fire's out, campers, so you can eat lunch in peace. Let's give thanks now for our safety!"

Upon their dismissal Becka got permission from Andrea to sit with Brad and his parents at lunch. Talk and clatter from other tables washed around them as Becka listened intently to Mr. Colton's Mississippi drawl. "When we got to Cabin 6 the fire was just getting a good start out back in the grass. I grabbed a broom and tried hitting the flames with it." Then he laughed. "Broke the broom to smithereens!"

"Cheap broom!" Brad said. "The fire doubled instantly."

"Cheap fire extinguisher!" his father echoed. "No pressure. So we unscrewed the top and poured it on the fire, but it continued to spread like crazy."

"Yeah," Brad agreed. "Some of us guys grabbed towels and soaked them in the sink and tried swatting the fire with them. Some other guys filled a trash can with water, and we finally got it put out with that."

"It was about twenty-five feet in diameter by then," his father reported.

"Yeah, but it didn't hurt Alec's cabin any," Brad said happily.

Becka glanced at Tricia, who seemed relieved, then across the room at Alec, whose face looked flushed.

"Did Alec get burned or something?" Becka asked. "He doesn't look too good."

"No," Brad replied. "He's coming down with some kind of flu. Felt pretty bad anyway. Then Rodney had to go and throw that firecracker out back and start the grass to blazing."

"Oh?" Becka raised an eyebrow. "The same Rodney from the pool that you like so much?"

Brad grinned. "The same one. And I still like him a lot. Just needs a little *molding*, that's all!"

Becka shook her head in disbelief. Brad certainly wasn't a quitter, and he possessed the rare ability to recognize the potential in the worst of his boys. She hoped, for Brad's sake, that the directors wouldn't send Rodney home. After all, firecrackers were strictly forbidden at camp.

Brad then told Becka and his folks about the two counselors who had passed out during the Waldensian Walk. "You know Wanda Hubbard, one of the other waterskiing instructors? Passed out cold! So did Lavonne."

Becka looked wary. "It's even hotter now. People will be fainting all over the place this afternoon at the Walk Through the Bible."

"I think we're going to stay in here for that," Brad said.

"I hope so."

The scenes from the life of the apostle Peter lost some of their charm without the real pond in the picture, but the staff did their best with makeshift props.

Becka, dressed in a brightly colored toga, announced her group's act with, "Welcome to the Sea of Galilee!" Then she

introduced the men in a "boat" and continued, "This is a nor-
mal day in the region, but something will happen that'll
change these men's lives." Then she took a deep breath and
hoped Joel remembered his cue. "Today Jesus of Nazareth is
walking down by the sea." She looked around. No Joel. All
eyes riveted on her while her heart beat faster. More loudly
she repeated, "Jesus of Nazareth is walking down by the sea."

In raced Joel, pulling on his robe and skidding to a stop in
front of her. Nonchalantly, he turned to the fishermen in the
boat and called them each by name.

Becka glanced at Brad, who grinned impishly at her. She
was looking forward to the evening with him and his folks.

When it came time for the walking-on-the-water scene,
Becka noticed that Alec was even more flushed than before.
He wasn't at all the dramatic, enthusiastic Peter he usually
portrayed. In fact, he could barely get through his lines.

"He's got a raging fever," Tricia whispered. "As soon as he
finishes here he's going to sack out at the nurse's station."

"I'm sorry," Becka whispered back.

The air didn't cool much with the setting sun, but the Colton car was air-conditioned, and everyone was in a jovial mood
as they drove into town.

Business was brisk at the restaurant they selected. Becka
ordered a zucchini and mushroom dish. While they awaited
their food, the Coltons gave their son a present—a new suit.

Brad looked quite pleased and hugged his mother.
"Thanks!"

Becka gazed over at Mr. Colton. He was a man who thrived
on bustle, big business, and the precision of his computers.
He, like Becka, loved to run—every evening after work. Suddenly he turned his attention on the girl. "Brad tells me I'm
supposed to be looking for a car for you."

Becka nodded in assent.

"Could you tell me what you're interested in?"

Becka didn't hesitate. "First off, it has to cost not much over
$2,000. That's all we've managed to save for it," she explained.

He gave her an appraising look, then flashed a knowing
smile at his wife.

"And," Becka continued, "it has to get good gas mileage."

"Quite a practical girl you've got here, Brad!" Mr. Colton declared.

"Don't let her fool you," his son retorted. "If she could afford it, she'd latch onto a gas-guzzling, cherry red sports car!"

Everyone laughed, including Becka. "Brad knows me well," she thought.

Later, wishing the evening could have lasted longer, she hugged a red balloon and waved to the Coltons from the front of her cabin.

Her girls were in the midst of their own party with cookies and pop abounding. Under her breath Eldora informed the counselor, "They're all getting along beautifully."

The assistant wouldn't have sounded so confident, though, could she have peered into the future to the following morning.

Chapter 6

Let Your Light Shine

Morning dawned silent, clear, and hot—again. Because staff worship was postponed until eleven o'clock on Sundays, Becka slept past her usual waking time. She didn't care that she missed the rising sun's buttery splash along the hilltops or the twitters of early birds. Today she could linger awhile in her bunk and awaken slowly. Wiping the sleepiness from her eyes, Becka yawned, stretched, and glanced at her campers. They, too, looked sluggish after the late-night party. It took only seconds for the counselor to feel the silent darts of hostility hurling between the two sisters and Carol and Cheryl.

"Not again!" she groaned inwardly, coming to life with an unwelcome abruptness, as if the four girls had thoroughly drenched her with a bucket of ice water.

Before any verbal explosions were allowed to rock her peaceful cabin, Becka consulted with Eldora about the situation.

The assistant sighed audibly. "Well, I guess we'd better confront them at once." Disappointment dragged at her words. "After the good time we all had at our party last night, I thought surely everything was patched up among them."

"I thought so too," Becka lamented. "Uh, let's handle this as a team, OK?"

"OK."

The two counselors entered the room together and rounded up the four girls.

"Campers," Becka began cheerfully, "Eldora and I have no-

46

ticed an unhappy spirit here this morning. Could you share with us what's going on?"

Fawn hesitated, glancing coldly at Carol and Cheryl, then complained, "The rest of the campers are hogging all the leftovers from the party."

"Yeah," Fern chimed in, "we gave money for some cookies, but Eldora couldn't find the kind we wanted. So she bought some other things instead. And now no one'll share their leftovers with us—just because we didn't get the kind of cookies we ordered."

Cheryl defended herself. "It's only fair that Carol and I get to keep the pop, even though there was a lot left."

Before Becka could respond, Eldora surprised her with, "Listen, girls! All week we've been learning about what real friendship is. We've been watching skits on how to become better friends and better Christians." Eldora faced Carol and Cheryl squarely. "Where have you two been, anyway? I don't mean to sound critical, but this looks like an example of pure selfishness to me."

Carol pushed her glasses back up on her pert nose. "Well, I guess it wouldn't hurt to give them our two bottles of root beer," she conceded.

Eldora eyed the pouting Cheryl. "Is that all right with you?"

The girl shrugged. "I don't like root beer much, anyway."

Fawn grabbed the bottles with a triumphant flourish and quickly stuffed them into her duffel bag.

Becka was speechless. Eldora had just proved there might be much more to her character than boys, makeup, and modern music. "My assistant could develop into an excellent counselor before the summer's over," she mused, regretting her earlier negative feelings about the girl.

By noon the last of the campers had left camp, and when the afternoon sun blazed its hottest, the last of the new crop of campers straggled over to the pool. Becka looked around quizzically. "Where are all the kids—especially the girls?" she wondered aloud.

"This must be it," Tricia said.

Becka squinted. "But there aren't enough to fill up even half the cabins."

Tricia looked unconcerned. "Oh, the directors will think of something. Come on!" she called out. "Let's practice turns."

Becka swam lightheartedly after her friend, lingering long in the cool water that sweltering afternoon. Later at supper, the mammoth lodge seemed to swallow up the meager group of juniors.

When her girls rose from the table to make their way to the food line, Becka heard Andrea's voice up front. "All girl counselors, please come to this end of the cafeteria."

Becka looked longingly at the steaming platters. She felt ravenous after so much swimming, but made her reluctant way across the lodge, as ordered.

The girls' director looked grim, her long hair straying here and there from the band at the back of her neck. "Because we don't have enough girls for full staff," she told them, "I need to ask seven of you to volunteer to return home during junior 2 camp. It'll mean earning only half-scholarship for the week."

Home! The word shot through Becka like an electrical charge. It was cherry harvesting time in the Columbia River Gorge. She could imagine the leafy orchards, their branches weighted down with clusters of dark red fruit. How she longed for the cool evenings and warm camaraderie of her family! Oh, if she could just board a plane and fly home for the week!

"Such nonsense!" she scolded herself, remembering how long her parents had saved for the car she would buy this summer. She considered the past two years, working part time at the college, helping with her school bill. "Only cherries grow on trees," she mused, "not hundred dollar bills!" And she sadly realized it would take well over three of those bills for plane fare to the Northwest.

Her assistant, Eldora, was the first one to volunteer. Other hands flew up, including that of Roxanne Dudley, a skiing instructor who worked with Brad. Becka looked on enviously, still thinking about the week of rest she craved. For three years she had done nothing but push, push, push herself.

Andrea's voice brought her back to reality. "We'll let you know after campfire tonight what your cabin assignments will be."

Eldora looked ecstatic. "Can't wait to phone Mom and tell

her the good news!" she exclaimed.

"I'm really glad for you," Becka said, then added a wistful, "What I'd give to fly home . . ."

Eldora's ecstasy quickly turned to despair, however. When Becka led her girls down to the Pecan Grove later for campfire, she found her assistant in tears, hiding behind a tree.

"What's the matter?"

"My mother can't come and get me," Eldora sobbed. "I'm going to have to go home with Roxanne, and I don't even know her."

"Brad says Roxanne's nice."

"But I'll be living in a house full of strangers for a whole week!" she cut in.

Becka digested her statement for a moment, then pointed out, "Everyone was a stranger to you here at El Camino Ranch, and you haven't had any problems with that."

"Well, at first I was sort of scared," Eldora sniffed.

"But then you quickly got to know many of us and weren't afraid anymore," Becka reminded her. "It'll be the same at Roxanne's home, you'll see."

"Think so?"

"Sure!" Suddenly Becka spotted Marelda, who had stayed on for junior 2 camp. She was traipsing over to the boys' section, seeking out her heartthrob, Carlo.

Eldora took in the scene also. "Good luck with Marelda this week!" She giggled in spite of her tears.

"Thanks! I'll need it," Becka replied, heading for the boys' section. "Marelda," she cooed, "it's time to start singing. Let's go back where we belong!" The counselor steered the dark-haired girl in the opposite direction.

"But—but—" Marelda sputtered, "Bert said I could visit Carlo."

"Bert's not your counselor. I am."

"Yeah, but he's one of your bosses." The younger girl twisted the words into a threat.

Her smile still in place, Becka gently pushed the girl onto a log. "Let's sing!" she said.

The guitars had begun, and the dusky air quickly filled

with children's voices. Becka gazed around, trying to find Brad among the boys, but she couldn't see him anywhere. She noticed his best friend Alec, though, leaning against a gnarled tree.

"Oh, good!" Becka thought. "Alec's back with us. Must be over the flu." But on closer observation, she realized Alec wasn't singing. In fact, he looked stony-faced.

"Maybe he's still sick," she speculated. When Eldora returned to her section, Becka slipped silently away.

Brad suddenly appeared from the other side of Alec.

"What's going on?" Becka asked.

"I want to go home—for good," Alec blurted.

"You mean, you're still sick?" she asked.

"Yeah," he replied grittily. "Sick to my stomach!"

Brad looked uncomfortable. "Alec had a bad experience at the nurse's station this afternoon," he explained.

Becka cocked her head questioningly as the juniors' swelling voices threatened to drown out his words.

Alec turned around, facing the sinking sun that glowed through the trees. "I've spent the last couple of days sprawled out on a cot in a sick room, you know."

Becka nodded.

"Well, four staff members, whom I'll leave unidentified, came in to visit someone else. They didn't know I was awake in the other room."

"Uh-oh!" Becka exclaimed. "And they said something unkind about you, huh?"

"Not just me, Becka, but about Tricia, you, and Brad, too! Lies! Bold-faced lies about how we've supposedly been sneaking out at night, etcetera, etcetera."

Becka glanced over at Brad's somber face while his friend stabbed the night air with a clenched fist. "And I don't want to work at a place that's supposed to teach Christian values when it's full of rattlesnake tongues!"

"Hold on!" Brad protested. "Four people do not a whole staff make. And you can't give the devil the satisfaction of using them to get you to quit!"

Alec considered the charge.

Becka could tell his stand was weakening, so she added, "And

Alec, if you quit, Tricia'll quit too. And I'd miss her terribly." With that she whispered to Brad, "Don't let him leave! I've got to get back to my girls. Marelda's getting restless."

The counselor took her tangled emotions back to her place at the campfire and tried to sort them out. "As careful as we've been about our examples to the campers, how could those people say such horrid things about us?" She, too, shared a touch of Alec's indignation.

She didn't realize how much Brad was affected by the gossip until the next evening when the couple ate together at a fast-food restaurant in town.

"I'm really glad to have a break," she told him. "That Marelda is getting more Carlo-crazy by the hour. And I've been switched from swimming to crafts, which I know nothing about."

Brad looked dazed, as if he hadn't heard a word.

"You talked Alec into staying," she said. "Why so grim?"

Brad looked down at his salad. "Well, I also feel bad about what those people said about us."

"Me too."

He kept inspecting the salad. "If I didn't have such strong convictions about certain things, those lies wouldn't bother me any."

"What kind of convictions?" Becka probed.

Color rose to Brad's face as his eyes locked on hers. "This may sound old-fashioned and corny, but I think it's just as important for a guy to keep himself pure for his bride-to-be as it is for a girl, her husband." He took a quick breath. "In fact, I want to wear a gleaming white tuxedo at my wedding someday for that very reason."

Relief spread across Becka's face. "That's not corny. That's beautiful," she told him. "I feel the same way." She stabbed a cherry tomato with a fierce vengeance, then waved it through the air like a baton. "And that's why those fibbers make me feel angry also."

Brad made a wry face. "It won't do any good to confront them about it. Alec already tried that."

"He did?"

Her boyfriend chuckled. "Yeah, at the nurse's station, right in the middle of their conversation. Alec saunters out and says, 'So Tricia and I have been sneaking out at night, huh?' "

Becka chortled, "You're kidding!"

Brad shook his head emphatically. "Alec said they turned scarlet from embarrassment. He had caught them red-handed."

Becka paraphrased the beatitude, "Blessed are ye when men shall revile you . . . and say all manner of evil against you" (Matt. 5:11).

Brad, a theology student, couldn't be outdone. "Let your light so shine before men, that they may see your good works, and glorify your Father which is in heaven" (Matt. 5:16).

Becka tossed back, "And let us make haste before we're late."

Brad frowned. "What's that? The gospel according to Becka?"

Later, as she sat among her girls at campfire, Becka thought dreamily about Brad and their conversation. For months their relationship had lingered in that vague area between "special friends" and "not-quite-engaged." They were talking more, sharing deeper thoughts. When one hurt, the other felt it. "He's such a sweet, sweet guy," she reflected, wondering where their friendship would lead them. Or would the end of summer bring an end to their relationship as well?

An image of Brad, the way he blushed, his gentleness, kept flitting through her mind, even after she had bedded down her girls.

Becka was in the kitchen, pouring herself a glass of water, when she heard a timid voice in the doorway, "I miss my mom."

"I do too," Becka said, spying chubby Coreen in pajamas. "Come over here and sit with me on the mattress awhile," she said, "and we'll talk about it."

Coreen tiptoed over to the mattress that sprawled alongside the kitchen wall, plopped down beside Becka, and began to talk nonstop. Her eyes brimmed with tears when she told how her father had died when she was small. Then she confessed how guilty she felt about leaving her mother at home. Becka simply listened and nodded from time to time.

At last Coreen stopped, looked around, then blurted, "And this kitchen looks just like our kitchen at home."

"Well, that settles it then," Becka said.

"What?"

"You're not allowed in this kitchen for the rest of the week!" the counselor teased.

Coreen giggled, hugged Becka's neck, then headed happily back to her room.

"What was that verse Brad quoted? 'Let your light so shine before men'? . . . before little girls," she mused. Moments like these made counseling worth all the heat, the separation from her family, and, yes, even the ants!

Only her side of the building, Cabin 14-A, was in operation that week. With Tricia and Eldora gone, Gwen Pennington had moved into her cabin. Gwen proved to be a capable counselor, helping Becka keep tight reins on Marelda. In comparison, the rest of the girls were angels, making her week as crafts instructor whiz by. Before she realized it, Sabbath afternoon had arrived and time for the Walk Through the Bible. They were back to The Pond for the life of Peter.

With Becka's scene completed, she followed the group around the water's edge. She loved to watch Brad as Jesus—and Alec as Peter, eager to climb out of his boat and walk on the water toward the Master.

Long ago Brad had shared his fears about the rickety, submerged dock he had to stand upon. Becka always held her breath until the scene was over. Today was no exception. She watched her boyfriend, balanced carefully on the unseen dock, walking majestically toward the boat that Alec and several others filled.

"It's a spirit!" one of them cried.

"I'm afraid!" called another.

"Be of good cheer!" Brad, as Jesus, commanded in a deep resounding voice. "It is I. Be not afraid!"

Alec stood up in the boat. "Lord, if that's really you, then bid me come unto thee on the water."

Brad dramatically stretched both arms forward. "Come!" he called.

Alec timidly swung his leg over the side of the boat, groping for the edge of the dock that wasn't there. "Row a little closer, apostles!" he ordered. His companions rowed a few strokes while a few wise campers snickered on shore. Then he dramatically lifted himself out of the boat and began to "walk on the water." At first he looked quite pleased, gazing into his Master's face. But then he scowled and eyed the pond fearfully. "The waves are so high," he exclaimed, then began to sink. "Lord, save me!" he cried.

"Oh, thou of little faith—" Brad began as he reached for Alec's hand. At that moment the dock must have tilted, because both "Jesus" and "Peter" plunged into the water, making an enormous double splash.

"Oh, no!" Becka gasped while campers screamed in delight around her.

Chapter 7

Brad's Turn for Trouble

Spluttering and grinning lopsidedly, the two actors emerged from the water and tried again. Alec crawled back into the boat, and Brad stood, with the soggy robe clinging in a twisted mass around him, and repeated his lines. This time the scene went according to the script.

Sunday morning Becka said goodbye to her juniors, and with immense relief watched Marelda bounce out of the cabin—for good. At the same time Eldora appeared, all smiles.

"You were right, Becka!" she said. "Roxanne and her family were terrific. In fact, Roxy and I have become best friends." Before Becka could reply, the words tumbled out, "I hope you don't mind, but we've asked Andrea if I can move in with Roxanne. Her assistant, Irene Dunn, can take my place here."

At first Becka felt too stunned to speak. She managed a bland smile, but her thoughts were elsewhere, all tangled in knots. She freely admitted to herself that she and Eldora hadn't shared the best of relationships. It was one of politeness and duty, but not particularly affectionate. Still, she had seen encouraging signs of growth in her assistant and had hoped, in time . . .

"Becka?" Eldora said questioningly.

Becka blinked herself back to the present. "It's fine with me, as long as the girls' director approves," she said.

"Great!" Eldora cheered, heading for her room to begin gathering her heap of belongings for the move.

Becka stared after her and felt cheated—cheated out of the

chance for a full-bloomed friendship with the younger girl. They had just begun to work as a team. "Oh, well," she consoled herself. "Sometimes people are so different they can't become really close, no matter how hard they try."

After lunch her new assistant, Irene, lugged two suitcases and a sleeping bag into Cabin 14-A. Becka greeted her warmly and showed her to her bed. The girl's face, ruddy with sunburn and a generous supply of freckles, grinned back appreciatively. Her hair encircled her head like a cumulus cloud of orange. Becka sensed at once that this girl would make an excellent helper.

Irene proved how capable she was when she took Becka aside at supper. "Molly, the nurse, just told me one of our girls has lice."

Becka felt her senses spin. She had never dealt with lice before. In fact, she didn't even know what a louse looked like. Her helplessness must have shown, because Irene patted her hand. "Don't worry, Molly has already taken care of shampooing the girl's hair and has disinfected her clothes."

"But what about her sleeping bag and other things?" Becka asked limply.

"I've taken care of this problem before," Irene assured her. "First, of course, it's important that none of the other girls know what's going on."

"Of course!" Becka agreed, realizing how devastating that knowledge would be to the poor girl's self-esteem.

Irene continued, "If you can take our campers to the program yourself tonight, I'll stay and wash all of the girl's clothes with some special detergent the nurse gave me."

"But how can you return from the laundry in time and still get all her things back where they belong?"

Irene thought a minute. "Could you linger awhile after campfire?"

"I'll do my best," Becka promised. Then she promptly sought out the camp director and asked him to dismiss her group last that evening.

Becka rejoined her nine teenagers at the dinner table and looked pleased with the lot. One by one they had arrived at the pool that afternoon, and she couldn't believe her good fortune. Not one "Marelda" in the group! She had quite a mixture of blonds and brunettes, some pudgy, one overly skinny, and every one of them smiley and sweet-natured. There were two Sarahs, a Bonnie, a Cora, a Tammy, Carla, Elaine, Christen, and Michelle. Now Becka could relax and enjoy counseling again.

At least she thought she could relax. Brad met her briefly at the food counter and made no effort to conceal his anxiety.

"I must have all the reform-school dropouts in my cabin," he said.

Becka glanced over at his table. They did, indeed, look like a surly group of thugs.

Under his breath he added, "And their ring leader, Dean Thomas, is out for revenge."

"What do you mean?"

"Last summer I caught Dean and a couple of kids sneaking away from the waterfront. He almost got tossed out of camp then. I guess he's still got it in for me, because life has not been pleasant since his arrival this afternoon."

In snatches throughout the meal Becka heard the entire story of Dean Thomas "and friends." Already, the tough-looking teenager with unsmiling eyes had shoved his face into Brad's and demanded, "Make me!"

"What did you do?" Becka asked.

Brad contemplated her question for a moment. "Well, truthfully," he admitted, "I felt like flattening his nose with my fist. But I reminded myself that I'm studying for the ministry, and I'm supposed to be a good example to these guys." He chuckled. "I think Dean realizes that, and it's the very reason he keeps badgering me, hoping I'll break and start something serious."

Thunder rolled across the sky as they talked, and Becka shivered at its timely interruption. "Brad, something tells me this week you may be facing some enormous tests of character." She shook her head. "And there's nothing I can do to help—except pray for you."

"Please do!" he said without any hint of humor.

A cloudburst sent Becka, Irene, and their nine girls scurrying back to the cabin and rest time.

Afterward the sun shone brightly and dried the Pecan Grove and surroundings for campfire that evening after supper.

"Don't forget to linger," Irene whispered to Becka as she left the cabin.

Her girls grew restless when the evening meeting ended. All the other groups but theirs were dismissed. When they were finally allowed to leave, Becka took the "scenic route." Still hoping to buy more time for Irene, she pointed out various landmarks with her flashlight. None of the girls acted impressed. After all, their first day of camp, combined with the long trip to get there, had taken their toll. Becka and nine very sleepy girls straggled back to the cabin. The counselor made as much noise as she dared at that time of night when she entered the building. "OK, girls!" she boomed. "Brush your teeth, and we'll gather for worship in my room." To herself she said, "And let's hope Irene had time to get back from the laundry."

Her assistant looked carefree, sprawled out on a bed, pretending to read a book. Her orange hair was a bit unkempt, but all bunks stared, mute and tidy, back at the counselor.

Becka breathed a quiet "Thanks!" and noticed a smug little smile on Irene's face.

The next morning Brad had a secret of his own. "I've gotten permission to search Dean's suitcase," he told Becka.

"Why?" she asked.

"Some of his threats may not be just hot air," he said. "Andy and I are suspicious and don't want to take any chances."

All morning Becka wondered about the search. Would Brad turn up anything? She looked forward to seeing him at lunch. But when she did, he seemed to have shrunk a little. There was a defeated sag to his whole body, and he couldn't take time to talk to her.

Escaping all ears during their break that evening, they drove into town, where Brad unloaded the day's events. "You'll never believe what I discovered in a very heavy cowboy boot in Dean's suitcase!" He paused. "A Smith and Wesson .38 caliber!"

Becka gasped. "You mean, a real gun—that shoots?"

"Yep! Found some bullets in another pouch, a radio, a few cigarettes, some sheets from a pornographic magazine, plus a nice, sharp knife."

Becka's voice came out weak and shaky as she repeated, "A gun? Oh, Brad!"

"The boys' director helped me search the rest of his stuff. We turned up no illegal drugs, but lots and lots of vitamins. Weird!" He took a deep breath. "I wanted the guy sent home immediately."

Becka felt incredulous. "You did?" Was this the same Brad who went to bat for Rodney when the youngster's firecracker nearly burned down the camp?

"I know that sounds contradictory," he said. "But Becka, Dean is different. He's not some harmless prankster, but a hard-core troublemaker. His language is worse than foul, and he's a terrible influence on the other guys in our cabin."

"What did the director say to your suggestion about Dean's leaving?" she asked.

"No," Brad replied flatly. "He says Dean needs to be exposed to the spiritual atmosphere here at camp. He hopes something might rub off on him."

"And meanwhile you and Andy will sleep with your eyes open," Becka said.

"You're right about that. I don't trust the guy one bit." Any amusement in Brad's eyes had died out. "We're talking real gun, real bullets, sharp knife."

All week Becka prayed for Brad and Andy's safety. She trembled at the sight of Dean and his "cronies" each time she saw them swaggering to line call with their I-don't-care-about-this-sissy-stuff expressions.

And every day Brad dragged more slowly up the hill to the lodge. Andy also looked worn out. The two counselors were taking a lot of fire, not just from their campers, but from the directors as well. Because their boys lived like hogs and the counselors couldn't get them to keep the cabin in order, the counselors caught the blame.

The week passed slowly, with an eerie tension growing inside Becka. She found herself praying for Brad and Andy at the oddest times, as if the angels might desert their posts unless she prayed. Praying made her feel better, but she still worried.

Whatever was happening behind the scenes, she found it hard to relax and enjoy the teen banquet on Thursday night. Some of her girls had dates for the occasion, and all of them dressed beautifully and hiked eagerly to the lodge that had been decorated in a Mexican theme. A large, star-shaped, multi-colored piñata hung in the center of the room. The climax of the evening arrived when the teenagers took turns blindfolded, swinging a bat at the piñata. It finally burst and everyone scrambled for the candy that scattered over the floor.

Even Becka managed to grab a few pieces. Her girls generously offered her some of theirs also. "I've really been blessed with these girls this week," she reminded herself, but then she worried about Brad for the thousandth time.

By Sabbath afternoon her boyfriend's eyes looked bloodshot and glazed with weariness. It seemed such an effort for him just to tell her, "Only one more night to go, but it's going to be a long one." Brad explained, "I overheard some of the guys plotting to sneak out tonight, so Andy and I plan to stay up and prevent that from happening."

"But, Brad!" Becka protested. "You and Andy are already about to drop. How can you ever stay awake?"

"We've got to." He spoke without bluster. "We can't allow guys like that to roam around camp after dark. There's no telling what kind of trouble they'd cook up."

He walked away slowly, leaving Becka to wonder. Could Brad and Andy face up to those guys if trouble broke out?

Chapter 8

Blind Camp

Brad and Andy looked barely conscious Sunday morning. Weariness showed in the dark circles under their eyes and the way they slumped heavily into their chairs at breakfast.

Later Brad brushed past Becka and whispered triumphantly, "Not a one escaped!"

She flashed him an approving grin, her tightly strung nerves relaxing a little. In an hour the "hoodlums" would leave El Camino Ranch, and her boyfriend could catch up on his sleep.

But at staff worship she noticed that Andy was missing. "He's got the stomach flu," Brad reported. "He's going home . . ."

She finished his sentence, "leaving you with a cabinful of sightless boys."

Brad nodded dully.

Becka tried to buoy his droopy spirits with, "Remember, this is our last week of camp. By this time next Sunday we'll have survived *and* earned part-scholarships to college."

He smiled wanly as Andrea interrupted their conversation. "Becka, your job for blind camp will be different."

"In what way?"

"Well, first off, you and Tricia will bunk together in 14-A without any campers."

Becka's eyebrows shot up. "No campers?"

"That's right, but you'll spend lots of time helping Tina with her cabin of little girls," Andrea explained.

"OK." No campers in my cabin! A week of sweet peace!

"You see," the girls' director continued, "there's only one cabin of young girls. The rest of the campers are older, much older."

"I understand."

"And I'll need you to help lead the totally sightless ones to various activities as well." She paused momentarily and looked at her clipboard. "And you'll be helping Wanda Hubbard in crafts all week instead of teaching swimming."

Becka made an effort to look cheerful about her newest assignment. But trading the cool waters of the pool for hours in the sauna-like crafts building sounded menacing. Now she was reminding herself instead of Brad, "Only one more week to go!"

Not long after that, blind campers arrived at El Camino Ranch in droves of every size and description. They were mostly adults in their twenties, though some were younger children; but they were all excited about their anticipated week in the wild.

Becka remembered her morning without contact lenses and how awful it had felt not to see, so when twenty-five-year-old Mason asked her to lead him around, she slipped her willing arm under his and led him carefully to the cafeteria.

That night after campfire she visited Tina's cabin and met her girls, all flitting from bunk to bunk like popcorn popping from a lidless pan.

Becka realized at once that mild-mannered Tina was no match for these spirited and spoiled youngsters. To make matters worse, all but one of them could see well enough to care for their own needs, but the rascals were taking full advantage of Tina's compassionate spirit and asking her to do menial tasks for them.

"It's only the first night," Becka thought in disgust, "and they're already running poor Tina ragged." She then encouraged each girl to dress herself in pajamas and gather for worship. It took about half an hour to settle them down for the story and prayer.

Afterward, however, bedlam broke loose again, and each camper used every tactic to stay awake one minute longer.

Eventually all the girls quieted down, and Becka left Tina alone with her charges.

A warm breeze fanned the cedars and oaks along the shadowy path as Becka walked back to her cabin. She found herself slowing briefly, awed by the moon, the quiet, and a few lights reaching out into the dark. "It feels so peaceful," she reflected, almost regretting her eagerness to leave the following weekend. "This hasn't all been work," she reminded herself, considering her friendships with Tricia, Alec, and, of course, Brad. She lost count of the campers she had counseled and seemed to help. She recalled their happy-sad faces when they left, their hugs, and their gratefulness. They were changed, somehow, and had taken a part of El Camino Ranch with them.

The next morning Becka marched into bedlam again as Tina, still in her nightshirt, tried feverishly to button, tie, and brush the hair of a dozen girls at once. Again Becka encouraged each camper to care for herself, which—after some coaxing—each did.

Becka found Tina's cabin calm, however, compared to the din at the crafts building. These weren't delicate little-girl voices resounding off the tin walls, but huskier, shriller, louder adult voices, all talking at once, clamoring for help around the plywood tables.

To complicate matters, three of the ladies spoke nothing but Spanish, and Becka's vocabulary in that language consisted of "buenos dias!" (good morning!) and "adios!" (goodbye!)—not much help in crafts. So she opted to guide their fingers through each step of the project. This took time—much time. All the while, the noise swelled so loud she thought the roof might lift off the building.

Becka giggled at the thought. A missing roof might help ease the oppressive heat inside the cramped place.

At lunch Tina was off helping Mason and his girlfriend eat at another table while her girls ran recklessly throughout the cafeteria like frolicking puppies. One by one Becka rounded them up and sat them down at their table, an exercise that proved fruitless. As soon as she left to round up others, a couple of the corralled ones escaped.

Finally, she asked Tina to help, then led them all to the kitchen, where they learned to stack trays. Hearing murmurs of discontent, she explained, "This job is to help get your attention, campers. Running around the cafeteria at mealtime is neither ladylike nor safe."

They finished their task, then descended the hill toward the cabin for quiet time. But their meek spirit was short-lived. Two renegades broke rank and sped ahead, disappearing in the distance. Becka, trapped at the side of a blind girl, couldn't leave her alone to chase after the others.

When the group entered the cabin, Becka caught a glimpse of four sneakers with legs attached under her bed. She smiled wickedly. "OK, campers, it's quiet time now. Everyone needs to rest and try to go to sleep." Then she added in an ominous voice, "If Louise and Lorry don't show up at once, I'm afraid they'll have to be disciplined."

Immediately one of the pairs of legs shot out from under the bed and Lorry shouted, "Boo!"

"Boo to you too!" Becka laughed. "I'm glad you decided to join us. "I hope Louise returns quickly also, before it's too late." But her words hung in the hot August air, unheeded.

Lorry eagerly scrambled onto her bunk, but all remained silent below. At first a smile grew on Becka's lips and stayed there. She found Louise's stubbornness amusing. But as the afternoon wore on and the heat intensified, her smile melted like wax. "With little air circulating under the bed, Louise must be roasting under there," she worried. She decided that perhaps she should venture a peek. Maybe the girl had passed out from heat exhaustion. More likely, Louise was hoping Tina would return and rescue her with, "Oh, you funny little girl!"

Becka squirmed inwardly, sensing Louise's quandary. The girl knew that the longer she waited to come out, the more severe her discipline would be. At the same time, she dreaded facing the consequences.

Just before Becka succumbed to her niggling conscience, she heard an eerie, ghost-like sound from under the bed, "Ooooo!" It wavered, bringing a tirade of giggles from the other girls.

Chapter 9

Heat Exhaustion

The corner of Becka's mouth twitched amusedly at Louise's stubborn yet comical behavior. It would be so easy to let the offending girl climb into her bunk and forget the promise of punishment. The very idea of spending her precious naptime on this spoiled child made Becka wilt.

But her conscience wouldn't let her take the easy way out. She knew that Louise needed—probably unknowingly craved—some discipline in her young life. Therefore, Becka gently fished the truant from under the bed and led her to the bathroom.

Gathering supplies, she singsonged, "Now you're going to clean this whole room."

"But I can't see good enough to clean this place," Louise whined.

"That's OK," Becka countered. "I'll tell you if you miss any dirt."

The younger girl folded her arms in defiance and stamped her tennis shoe on the floor. "But I don't *want* to clean the bathroom!"

"Louise," Becka said, "you deliberately ran ahead of the group against orders, and then you refused to come out from under the bed." She slipped her arm around the stiff shoulders. "I'm responsible for you, Honey, but I couldn't leave Mary alone and run after you and Lorry. What if something bad had happened to you two before I could get back to the cabin?"

Louise's mouth opened speechlessly, then shut again. So Becka continued, "For your safety and that of the other girls, you must mind me and stay with the group. Maybe this experience here will help you to remember." She handed her some spray cleanser and a cloth. "Now shoot some of this into the sink and scrub it with this rag."

Louise made a face, but obeyed. When she finished she said, "There! Now I can go lie down."

"Not yet," Becka said. "Next is the shower."

"But the shower's so big, and I'm so small!"

Becka steered her to the shower stall and guided her hand and rag over every inch of the tiles till they sparkled. "Thank you, Louise! You're a great help."

"Now can I go lie down?"

"But, Louise," Becka retorted, "you've been lying under my bed for a long while, gathering strength for this job. Next is the toilet."

The younger girl gulped the air and sputtered, "B-but I can't stand cleaning toilets."

Becka uttered some sympathetic murmurs while pouring cleaning solution into the bowl. She helped Louise hold the brush and swab out the toilet.

"Oh, yuck, yuck, yuck!" Louise blustered, "I'm going to throw up."

"Well, you're standing in just the right spot for that." Becka grinned at her own ingenuity, suspecting that this was probably the first time little Miss Louise had cleaned anything. "Now here's the spray bottle. Next you need to polish the outside of the bowl."

Silently defiant now, the girl sank to her knees and started the task. Meanwhile, Becka used the opportunity to check the rest of the cabin. The other campers lay as soundless as the few feathery clouds that drifted across the afternoon sky. Becka could almost hear their collective thinking, "Please, don't make us clean anything!"

Next Becka gave Louise a broom and helped her sweep the bathroom floor. All the while the girl protested, "I'm so tired. I have to lie down before I faint."

Becka ignored her and fetched a wet mop.

The girl crinkled up her face in disgust. "But I've never mopped before!"

"Good!" Becka replied pleasantly. "You'll learn something new then." Again she helped Louise guide the handle around the room.

At last the entire bathroom glistened, and Becka beamed. "Oh, Louise! The place looks beautiful. Thank you so much for your help!"

A mixture of emotions chased across the youngster's face. Obviously, she couldn't decide whether to be mad, sad, or glad.

Becka put a tall glass of cool water into Louise's hand and watched her drink thirstily. In moments both were back on their bunks, Becka wishing for an hour to nap instead of only ten minutes. She sighed, though, feeling satisfied. "Perhaps the child has learned something today," she mused. "And maybe these girls will mind and really enjoy the rest of their week at El Camino Ranch."

Louise wasn't finished trying Becka's endurance, however. The next afternoon during quiet time, just as Becka was settling down, a Barbie doll sailed past her bunk and *kerplunked* on the floor beside her.

A fit of giggles erupted above.

Becka reached down and grasped the doll. "Louise," she said in her most patient voice, "your doll seems to have slipped off your bed." As she returned the toy to its owner, she warned. "Watch her carefully, because if she falls again, she will stay on the floor until quiet time is over."

Becka dived back on her pillow, but before she closed her eyes, Barbie sailed past again. *Kerplunk*! Next Becka spotted two bare feet edging down the end of the bunk.

"Where are you going?" the counselor asked.

"To get my doll."

"I'm sorry, but you're not."

"But I can't sleep without my Barbie!"

"It's true," piped up Lorry from across the aisle. "She can't sleep without her Barbie."

Becka rolled over on her side, took a deep breath, and said, "Louise, I warned you that if your doll slipped off your bed again she would have to stay on the floor until quiet time is over."

"But I can't sleep without my Barbie!" the girl repeated, this time in a mournful wail.

Becka's thoughts whirled. Louise had stolen her nap the day before, and now she was trying for a repeat performance today. With the heat sapping her strength, she felt exhausted. She was tempted to let Louise have her way, give her back the doll, and ignore her. "But would that help the girl?" her conscience asked. Becka knew the answer. Consistency. She must hold to her word.

"No, Louise," she stated firmly. "You have a good view of your doll from up there. Look at her all you like, but stay in your bed!"

"I'm going to throw up without my Barbie!" came the threat from overhead.

"If you do, then you'll clean up the mess," Becka said, adding with a lilt, "I know what a good cleaner you are."

Again and again, with Lorry egging her on, Louise pleaded for her doll, making Becka feel more like an ogre by the minute. All the while she knew her precious rest time was slipping away like leaden sand in an hourglass. The final blow fell when the younger girl screamed, "If I can't get my doll, I'm going to spit on you!"

Becka felt her cheeks flush and sent up a quick, silent prayer for extra love and kindness. Then in an overly controlled voice, the counselor said, "Louise, the other bathroom hasn't been cleaned yet. Maybe you need some more practice."

Not another word was uttered. No pleases, no threats, just sweet, sweet quietude—and sleep, however brief.

Becka awoke abruptly to her alarm, staring into the miniature face of Barbie, who still gazed blissfully at the ceiling.

"OK, campers!" Becka called. "It's time for your afternoon classes." She laid the doll next to its owner without a word.

Apparently, Becka had passed Louise's final test, because the rest of the week went by more smoothly. Even the other girls seemed cooperative, although they did continue to take advantage of Tina's compassionate spirit.

Becka wished her tenure in crafts would end. With each day the temperature soared even higher, turning the tin building into an oven. She wondered about the new baby that had just been born to Marlena and Bert that week—another boy. *What a cruel welcome, this heat*!

By Friday morning the two fans in the crafts building whirred fruitlessly. It was subtle at first, when Becka began to react to the heat. Her hands felt as if they were trembling under their skin. Nausea gripped her stomach, and the roomful of noisy campers began to spin.

"Wanda," she said, her voice echoing hollowly in space as if someone else were talking, "something's the matter with me. I feel, uh—strange, and, and I think I'd better see the nurse."

Wanda looked deflated. "Don't tell me you're going to get sick and desert me too?"

Becka hesitated only a moment. "I'm sorry," she breathed, forcing out the words. "I've got to visit the nurse."

Stumbling out of the door, she blinked in the dazzling sunlight and pointed her feet in the direction of the nurse's station. The nausea came in waves now, and her skin felt red hot. The world around her blurred and tilted. But a locked door met her at the nurse's station. A note fluttered in front of her face, but she couldn't read it. Her eyes refused to focus. She groped in her pocket for a pen, then scrawled on the paper, "SICK—AT STAFF LOUNGE—BECKA."

She longed to crumple into a heap there on the porch and wait, but something kept urging her, "Get water! Get water!" She felt desperate, as if her very life depended upon it.

When she headed out again, this time to the staff lounge, she remembered Katrina collapsing at line call, then the other counselors who had passed out during the Waldensian Walk. Remorse swept through her when she recalled how she had judged those girls as "weaklings." She would never let a little heat get the best of *her*—so she had thought.

"Ha!" the sun seemed to taunt her from the sky. "You'll never make it! I've got you now!"

Her legs felt like concrete. She had to urge them to move. Step by step, bit by bit, she lumbered across the campground and into the deserted lounge. Everything was whirling.

The sink. A glass. Water. Cool, sweet water trickled down her throat. Another glass. She could feel the air-conditioning now. She lay down in front of a vent and dozed off.

"Becka!" It was the nurse's voice somewhere far away. "Becka, I've brought you some Gatorade and salt tablets." The nurse stuffed a thermometer between her teeth and felt her pulse. "Too much heat, huh?"

"Geth tho!" Becka lisped around the glass stick in her mouth.

Next the nurse urged her to drink. "Can you sit up?"

"Uh-huh." The girl struggled to a sitting position and washed the salt tablets down with the tasty liquid.

"No more tin buildings for you today!" the nurse ordered as she scrutinized the gauge on the thermometer. "You're suffering from heat exhaustion."

"But Wanda needs help in crafts," Becka murmured.

"Maybe this afternoon you can lounge at the pool or waterfront, but you need to stay cool. Here!" the nurse said. "Some extra salt tablets for later on."

Becka slept intermittently in the staff lounge until she felt able to hike up to the cafeteria. In the parking lot she bumped into Angela Wright, who worked at the waterfront with Brad. Explaining her situation, Becka asked Angela if she could help in crafts that afternoon while Becka took her place at the waterfront.

"Sure!" Angela replied. "I've worked in crafts before. If it weren't for the heat, I'd rather help teach crafts any day."

Becka smiled weakly, thinking Angela had been appropriately named indeed.

That's how Becka spent her last Friday afternoon at El Camino Ranch—near Brad. She helped a group of blind adults learn how to boat and slalom ski, a special wide waterski that, except for the fin underneath, resembled a small surfboard. The cool waters of the lake seemed to revive the girl as she kept hold of two women near the dock.

All went well until about four-thirty, when Brad belly flopped behind the ski boat. Rubbing his neck, he headed toward the shore. Alec took over, demonstrating how to slalom ski to those who were partially sighted. But Herb Wheatley, the pilot of the ski boat, became overly exuberant with his driving, zeroing in on the dock. Becka guessed that he wanted Alec to spray the campers, but Herb was approaching too fast.

"Get back! Get back!" Brad shouted to the campers in the water. They, with their guides, quickly splashed a retreat. Brad, who was further out, began to swim feverishly toward them.

Becka gasped. The boat had jerked off its threatening course, but Alec, on the slalom ski, with its knife-like fin underneath, was heading straight for Brad's skull.

"Watch out!" she screamed.

Chapter 10

Summer's End

Becka stared speechlessly as Brad thrust himself out and over into a deep dive just as the slalom ski sliced the water overhead. She noticed that Alec's tan had turned strangely gray, and she saw horror frozen on his face as he slowed and sank into the water.

Becka thought she waited hours for the sight of Brad emerging from the water—unharmed. With a gusty sigh she exclaimed, "He's all right!" then relaxed her hold on the two blind ladies flanking her.

They murmured sounds of relief while Becka watched Alec swim frantically back to Brad.

"Oh!" Alec gasped, and then he gripped Brad in a big bear hug. "Thank the Lord you're all right! I just knew that fin would split your head right down the middle!"

Becka was grinning with undiluted pleasure, but her knees still quivered. She felt as watery as the lake around her, like a spectator at a drama, only this drama was real, and the actors were her best friends.

Brad's head cocked to one side and he rubbed his neck. "I'm OK, but when I bellyflopped back there, I must have twisted something. My neck sure is sore."

"Well," Alec chortled, "that's better than having no head left on top of it!"

Brad's eyes mirrored his buddy's mirth. "I suppose!"

With the excitement over at the waterfront, everyone headed back to their cabins.

Later, while strolling through the last of the lingering dusk, Becka thought nostalgically about her days at El Camino Ranch. Although in some ways the negatives seemed to outweigh the positives, there were still a lot of good times to tuck away in her memories. Best of all, her special friendship with Brad had not only survived, but it had grown deeper and more meaningful that summer.

The next morning Becka's pulse quickened when Andy and Alec showed up at staff worship without Brad.

"His neck's in bad shape," Alec said. "The director asked me to take him to the hospital later."

"Again?" Becka wondered about this accident-prone boyfriend of hers.

Alec continued, "Because you're not a counselor-in-charge this week, Luke said you could go along if you like. I'll be leaving right after church."

"I like," Becka quipped, and later she sat behind Alec and a very subdued Bradley Colton on the way to town.

When they arrived at the hospital, she and Alec settled into some cushiony, vinyl-covered chairs outside the emergency room and waited.

"Well, if this weren't blind camp, the Waldensian Walk would be starting about now," Alec said, then added with mock sincerity, "I'm sure going to miss it."

Becka was more truthful. "Not me! And I'm glad Mack had the sense not to try to lead all those campers through the hills." She frowned. "I mean, the Waldensian Walk was hard enough on us sighted people."

Alec nodded, and he seemed to note Becka's distracted look. "Thinking about Brad, aren't you?"

She smiled. "Of course!"

"Don't worry!" he assured her. "There wasn't any numbness or tingling in his arms and fingers. His neck isn't cracked, just probably badly sprained. It's one of the hazards that goes with being a waterskiing instructor."

"I know." Becka hesitated. "Brad has certainly gotten hurt a lot this summer, hasn't he?"

"That's just part of our job, Ma'am." Alec drawled the words like a dedicated old-West sheriff. He was acting most paternal, which seemed odd for a teenager—"but very sweet," Becka decided.

In his regular voice, he said, "I'll have to find someone to take Brad's place for our Walk-Through-the-Bible scene this afternoon."

"Yes," Becka replied. "But at least it'll be easier, because we'll perform in the cafeteria instead of at The Pond."

"True," Alec laughed. "We won't have to worry anymore about toppling into the drink. What a relief!"

For Alec's sake, Becka managed to giggle. Still, she worried about her boyfriend. Would he be able to drive the lengthy trip back to his home the next day? Brad's parents had invited her to stay with them for the two weeks before college resumed, and her own mother planned to drop by the Coltons' on her way back from a trip to her parents' place on the East Coast. Becka sighed, wishing she could see her father, too, but he would be busily trucking logs to an Oregon mill, making money to help keep her in college and her brother in academy. She would see him at Christmas.

About noon Brad lumbered into the waiting room. As Alec had predicted, the X-rays revealed no cracked or chipped bones. His neck had suffered a bad whiplash, however, and the doctor had given him some potent pain medication that, he said, would make him groggy. The threesome then returned to the ranch.

At the end of Sabbath that night, Andrea handed Becka a long checklist. "Here are all the chores that need to be done in Cabins 14-A and B before you and the other counselors can leave tomorrow."

Becka scanned the list briefly. "OK," she replied. "Uh—because we don't have any campers in our cabin, would it be all right if Tricia and I start on this list tonight?"

"Sure!" Andrea said. "I'll be by sometime after ten in the morning for inspection."

The thought of going home to Brad's house for a two-week vacation gave Becka the extra surge of energy she needed to lug a bulky vacuum cleaner from the headquarters building all the way to her cabin. She immediately attacked the list of chores by vacuuming the entire building. Then she mixed a solution of disinfectant and water in an oversized bucket and began to wash all the plastic mattress covers. Tricia did the same on her side of the building. Next they packed as many of their belongings as they could into their suitcases and a few extra boxes. It was after midnight when they began the tedious job of defrosting and cleaning out the refrigerator.

"I feel so tired I could sleep right here on the bottom shelf," Tricia sighed.

"Me too!" Becka agreed. "But just think how much we've finished on the list!" she pointed out. "And tomorrow we can start home early."

"Home!" Tricia breathed the word like a prayer. "I can play Mother's little girl for a while instead of feeling like a mother myself all the time."

"I'm afraid I've felt more like a *warden* most of the summer," Becka admitted lamely, "especially this week, trying to keep Louise and her crew in line."

"Ew!" Tricia interrupted. "This refrigerator's a mess."

"Sure is!" Becka said. "I've never defrosted a freezer compartment before, but this is a good time to learn."

"At midnight? You're kidding!" Tricia started washing the gooey racks and shelves.

An hour later she asked Becka's permission to go to bed. After all, the other two counselors in their building had retired long before.

"Certainly!" Becka replied. "Thanks so much for your help, Tricia! You're a true friend." Becka frowned at some stubborn ice still clinging to the underside of the freezer. "This stuff should drop off any second now."

She was wrong. It took an hour-and-a-half longer to dissolve all the "icebergs." Meanwhile, she made good use of her spare moments by scouring the stove top, including the wells of the four burners, until it sparkled like a newly bought appliance.

At two-thirty she went to sleep, waking what seemed only minutes later, at seven. Her eyes fuzzy with fatigue, she dragged herself through the morning ritual of showering and dressing. Then, sticking to her objective, she quickly started polishing the insides of all the windows in the building.

Tricia called from one of the bathrooms she was cleaning, "We'll leave the outside of the windows, the oven, the kitchen floor and cupboards, and the last bathroom for Gwen and Irene to do."

"If that's OK with them!" Becka called back deliberately loud, hoping the other counselors heard her. She mumbled to herself, "They aren't acting very inspired about work this morning." In fact, Gwen and Irene were sprawled on a mattress in the kitchen, boxing cereal cartons back and forth.

When she finished cleaning another bathroom, Becka reported to Andrea for her special assignment, which was to pick up all the litter that had found hiding places in grooves and grass near the cafeteria.

Most of their blind campers had left by then, and Becka began to feel something like the way she felt cleaning out her desk on the last day of school. There was sadness in saying goodbye to her good friend Tricia, and to Alec and the others she had grown fond of. She hoped to get a glimpse of Marlena's new baby boy and witness one more smile from his older brother. Then there would be elation and relief, knowing her job was finished and she had earned a part-scholarship for her junior year of college.

When she finished the trash detail, Becka got permission to enter the boys' village and help the ailing Brad load his car. Just as she hauled a final suitcase to the Mustang, Tricia appeared, her face flaring. "I can't believe it! Gwen and Irene said they won't finish the list, that we're going to have to finish it ourselves."

Becka felt as if her friend had just punched her squarely in the stomach. "What?"

But Tricia hadn't finished. "They talked to Andrea and accused us of taking all the easy jobs." Her pale eyes filled with tears. "And that's not the worst of it," she sobbed. "Gwen has told the rest of the girls that you and I haven't been much help all summer, that our attention has been solely on Alec and Brad. And n-now," she stammered, "no one's talking to me."

Becka frowned as she hugged her friend. She felt too stunned to speak. Tricia apparently felt the same, because for a time they just stood staring into space, a small, gloomy silence between them. Finally, Becka said, "It can't be that bad."

"It is," Tricia countered. "I know a cold shoulder when I see one. And that's what everyone's giving me this morning."

"Mmmm!" Becka murmured thoughtfully, her emotions see-sawing between hurt and anger. She fought them by trying to analyze the situation objectively.

"Listen, Tricia, Gwen and Irene are just as tired as we are. Blind camp is stressful anyway—lots of added responsibilities. Don't you think they might be trying to find any excuse to cop out of their chores because they're just plain beat?"

"Maybe," Tricia sniffed. "But it's terribly unfair. We were up half the night."

That recollection reduced the girl to fresh sobs, and Becka's arm returned to her friend's shoulder. "Don't I know it!" she exclaimed. "I think this all boils down to a big communication gap." Becka made a clicking sound with her tongue. "We should have consulted Gwen and Irene last night *before* we plunged into the chores."

"But they weren't there!" Tricia protested. "They were with the campers."

"That's just it," Becka said. "They didn't see all we had accomplished before they returned last night. Then they slept through most of the rest of it. I think if we had consulted with them first, none of this would have happened."

"Perhaps you're right." Tricia blew her nose. "Just the same, I want to leave this place as soon as I can. At the moment I feel like one of those lepers in the New Testament."

Becka's earlier generous feelings for El Camino Ranch had all but faded. She was suddenly very weary of responsibility in general. Like Tricia, she would love to skip back to girlhood and be mothered awhile also—just long enough to get fortified for her role in adult society again. Sometimes society could be awfully cruel.

All of a sudden Brad hobbled out onto the porch like an eighty-year-old man in the advanced stages of arthritis.

"Your boyfriend's in bad shape, isn't he?" Tricia whispered.

Becka nodded. "It's the medicine. The pain's so bad he can't do without it, but with it he's terribly groggy." Then she voiced her deepest fear, "I don't know how he's going to drive us home today."

Minutes later, she and Tricia followed Andrea around the cabin while the girls' director inspected the premises.

Becka gasped when she opened the bathroom door to discover a dead roach in the middle of the floor, his short stiff legs aimed at the ceiling. "Honestly, he wasn't there when I left!"

Tricia defended her. "I'm sure he was just waiting to run out there and die when she finished cleaning—some sort of revenge!"

Andrea gave them the tiniest flicker of a smile while Becka used a tissue to discard the bug.

Next came the windows. "Only the insides are done," said Tricia weakly.

"But if we have to polish the outsides too, we will," Becka offered. "Anything to get on the road."

Andrea blinked blankly. "Windows? What windows?" She turned to both girls and told them with earnestness, "You've done more than your share. You're free to go."

Now tears nearly swelled out of Becka's eyes—appreciative tears. Maybe society wasn't so cruel after all.

Something was lingering in the hot desert air that hung heavily over El Camino Ranch. Something mischievous. Already, some anonymous fellows had wrapped Mack Nolan's car with streams of toilet paper. Although Brad felt sluggish, he and Alec could not leave camp without playing a trick on the biggest prankster of all, Herb Wheatley, the driver of the ski boat that nearly cost Brad his head.

Waiting expectantly with two plump water balloons outside the cafeteria, Alec and Brad hurled them on target at Herb when he came through the door.

Growling and grinning at once, Herb took off for the fire station.

"Uh-oh!" Alec exclaimed. "Something tells me he plans to spray us with the fire hose."

"This is a good time to leave, wouldn't you say?" Brad asked innocently.

"But Tricia's and my stuff!" Becka cried.

"Hurry!" Alec ordered, hopping into his pickup. Brad followed with the two girls in his car to Cabin 14.

Becka could hear the fire truck grinding down the hill toward them.

Tricia was racing out of the building with a final load when she screamed, "Quick, Becka! If he sprays my things, they'll all be ruined."

Becka made a final visual sweep of her empty cabin, then ran for Brad's car.

Dust stirred in the wake of the approaching fire truck. Glancing over her shoulder, Becka spotted the oversized Herb jump from the cab and go for the firehose at the rear. He had had time to think vengeful thoughts and was all muscle and fury now. He unfurled the hose and planted his bulky frame behind the nozzle, aiming it threateningly at both vehicles, like a soldier behind an antitank gun.

Chapter 11

The Silver Renault

Squealing tires sent the pickup lurching ahead, while Brad yanked his transmission into gear and followed hastily. Both vehicles careened down the hill.

Becka glanced back again at Herb, who fumbled with the valve on the limp fire hose. "Whew!" she breathed. "That was close." Then she realized that her good friends were escaping without a proper goodbye.

"Oh, Brad!" she moaned. "I didn't get to hug Tricia. She's been like a sister to me this summer."

"Don't worry!" he said. "The four of us are meeting at the Mexican restaurant just inside the city limits. I arranged it all before we left."

They did meet, they ate, and they parted with hugs and promises to write. Then Alec's pickup headed across the intersection while Brad's Mustang pulled into the southward-bound line of traffic. Brad drove pensively, misery dragging at his eyes.

"This medicine is making me so sleepy," he complained, "I can hardly stay awake." He looked at Becka. "Do you think you could drive for a while?"

"Through the city—in this traffic?" she asked in a meek voice. "What if I hurt your sweet little Mustang?" She stroked the dashboard as if it were her calico cat, Potluck. "I'd never forgive myself."

Abruptly, Brad twisted the steering wheel, turning into a restaurant parking lot.

"Where are you going?"

"For the shade of that tree!" he said. "I'm sacking out."

"But we'll roast in this heat!"

"That's better than dying in a wreck," he retorted. Opening the door, he crawled into the back seat. No sooner had Becka rolled down the windows than she realized her boyfriend was snoozing soundly—unconscious of the heat, the traffic, or the flies buzzing in and out of the car.

She leaned back and reflected on summer events and on all that would happen in the next few days. Her mother would be driving through the Southwest in a few days. "It'll be good to see Mom," she mused. Becka was also eager for her mother to meet Brad's parents. Brad himself had already met her family when he had flown to the Northwest in May. Furthermore, she hoped Mr. Colton had found her a car by now, so she could drive it back to college.

The minutes ticked into an hour, but Brad didn't stir. Edgy with waiting, Becka fretted. They had a long trip ahead of them, and it was already well past noon. Then out of weariness and boredom she, too, dozed off.

When she awoke later, their shade had vanished, and her skin felt sticky all over. She glanced at the back seat. "Brad!" she whispered gently. "Do you want me to go in here and buy us some iced juice or pop?"

He mumbled something unintelligible, which she assumed meant "yes," and set out on her errand. The cold air conditioning surged around her like a refreshing breeze, and she lingered as long as she could before venturing out into the heat again.

When she returned, Brad was sitting in the front seat, blinking blearily at the afternoon. "I can't believe I've slept so long," he yawned.

"I slept too," Becka said as she handed him his drink. "Rough night of cleaning!"

"Ow!" Brad groaned, grabbing the back of his neck. "The medicine must be wearing off."

Becka winced, then tried, "If you can get us through the city, I'll take over the wheel once we're out in the country."

"I'll do my best," Brad promised, turning the key. "Let's

turn on the air and get this car cooled down inside."

Becka fastened her seat belt and smiled. They were on their way again.

But the stop-and-go traffic persisted for miles, as if the stop-lights were part of a grand conspiracy to trap the couple and never let them out of the city. Uncomplainingly, Brad kept his head as straight as possible and pretended that he wasn't in dire pain.

When they finally emerged from a last snarl of road construction and helter-skelter detours, Becka looked at open space, and miles of gentle rolling hills in every direction.

"We made it!" she sighed, as she unstrapped her seat belt. "I can take over now."

Brad didn't argue. He pulled off the road and surprised her by walking around to her side and opening the door.

"Even in such misery, he's still a gentleman!" she thought, and she flashed him her most appreciative smile. But he didn't seem to notice. He flopped back down in the back and was asleep again in seconds.

Becka's pulse raced with anxiety as she readjusted the mirrors and seat. "He's so trusting!" she mused. Unsure of her ability to drive with a stick shift, Becka silently gathered her wits.

The car's jerky start back onto the road smoothed out once she got it into high gear and aimed southeast on the two-lane highway. She drove slower until she gained more confidence. Her only hurdles lay in the few small towns with their twenty-five-mile speed zones, when the car jerked a bit, but with practice she got better. At about five that evening she heard a voice from the back seat. "Where are we?"

Becka giggled. "Somewhere between Canada and Central America! And how are you feeling?"

"A little better, I think," Brad said. "But my stomach feels empty. Are you hungry too?"

"I haven't thought much about it, but I must be."

"Good!" He leaned forward over the seat so they could see each other better. "In the next town let's look for a restaurant."

A half-hour later they sat across from each other at a table.

Brad had washed up in the restroom and looked more present-able. Becka noticed that some cheerfulness had seeped back into his manner.

"This trip is stretching into a lengthy one," he said with a yawn.

"It couldn't be helped," she replied. "Do you think your parents will worry?"

"Not until midnight. Then, I guarantee you, they'll send out the troops."

Becka's eyes widened. "Surely, we'll get there long before that!"

"About sunset, I'd guess." Brad's smile had lost its brilliance, but it was still there, cheering her. "Thanks, Becka! I know how anxious you were about driving my car." He ate a little more, then said, "It really isn't safe for me to be behind the wheel, so I'll have to presume upon you all the way to my house."

Becka tried to look brave. "I might get lost once we turn off this main highway."

"Don't worry! I'll guide you in," he assured her.

As the sun set behind spindly pines, the faithful Mustang wended its way through the forest lands above Houston, and Becka relaxed. Brad was sitting next to her now. She could feel his eyes studying the profile of her faace.

"Well, we survived," he told her gently.

"We're not quite home yet."

"I mean, our relationship survived the summer at El Camino Ranch," he said.

"Oh, it got a little shaky on occasion." She grinned at him.

"That it did," he agreed. "But the important thing is that we weathered those occasions, and it's stronger because of them."

"Think so?"

"Uh-huh." Then he asked, "Do you realize, when November comes we'll have been dating for one year? November 21, to be exact."

Becka sobered. "Do you think we'll still be together then?"

"I'm sure of it."

They turned onto the bumpy road that led to the Colton house. Around the next bend it waited, a large, white Victorian manor. Its windows cast golden shafts of light out into the dusk, welcoming them.

When she parked the car and turned off the motor, Becka breathed a prayer of gratitude. The night was windless and warm. No voices, no hum of faraway traffic, just the soft serenade of crickets and frogs.

In moments they were greeted by the outstretched arms of Brad's parents and were sorting out the news: the skiing accident, their hasty departure, the tortuous journey home, then the car Mr. Colton had found for Becka, and Mrs. Bailey's anticipated arrival on Friday. They sat in the comfortable living room with a vista of the darkening pine forest through every window.

Aware of their tremendous fatigue, Mrs. Colton called the visiting to a halt and guided Becka to the guest room. The drapes, the valance, the puffy bedspread, the carpeting, all matched in the muted hues of pale sunflowers. There Becka slept soundly and dreamed of endless highways, hills, and traffic lights.

A great deal of life went on in Mrs. Colton's kitchen, and the week sped by quickly, full of her delectable Southern cooking—grits, cornbread, and vegetarian dishes that made Becka's mouth water.

She and Brad helped with the dishes and with other household chores. By Thursday his neck felt well enough for him to head outdoors to a daylong lawn-mowing session. Becka cheered him on from the shady porch that wrapped halfway around the house. She thought how much like a storybook setting this was.

That evening Mr. Colton took them to an automobile dealership in town and showed them the little silver Renault he had found. "It's $2,400, in excellent condition, and they'll even throw in brand-new, steel-belted radials for the price."

Becka's heart sang when she examined the car. "It's darling!" she exclaimed. She sat inside and noticed how new it looked. Very little mileage showed on the odometer. Definitely a good buy, she decided. She felt grateful for Mr. Colton's help, since her own father wasn't there to advise her.

She tried to act cool and businesslike, but "I love it!"

blurted out and spoiled her act. "Now if Mom will approve it tomorrow, it'll be mine."

Her mother did approve the following afternoon, and in the midst of a thunderstorm, papers were signed and the all-important check written. Becka's spirits soared so high she felt as if she were flying an airplane back to the house instead of her little silver car.

That Sabbath was full of warmth, worship, chatter, and more delicious food. Mrs. Bailey and the Coltons visited as easily as if they had been neighbors for years. And Becka's mother was especially impressed with how considerately Brad treated his mom.

"Has he always acted this way?" she asked Mrs. Colton.

"As a matter of fact, he has," the other woman replied. "Brad has been such a blessing—even when he was small."

Later, in the privacy of the guest room, Mrs. Bailey told her daughter, "I've heard that one can usually tell the character of a man by the way he treats his mother. Why, Brad is the sweetest, most attentive son I've ever seen!" She wagged her finger in Becka's face. "You keep this guy, understand?"

Becka beamed. "I hope to."

After an hour of looking through photo albums, Mrs. Bailey kissed her daughter, thanked the Coltons heartily for their hospitality, and bid everyone goodbye.

"I miss your father so much," she intimated to Becka as they strolled to the car. "I want to arrive home by Thursday so our reunion on Sabbath will be a special one with a clean house and some wholesome meals." She uttered a sound of disapproval. "No telling what kind of bachelor food he's been eating while I've been gone!"

One last hug and "I love you, Sweetheart!" and her mother drove away.

With a day's excursion to the beach and more yard work, the final week of summer vacation seemed to evaporate. Early Sunday morning Becka and Brad packed their respective cars for the trip back to college. After Mrs. Colton reminded Becka to "buckle up," the girl thanked her host and hostess again for the stay and put her car in gear, carefully following the Mustang out of the driveway.

Leaving the curvy roads, the two cars picked up speed on a straight stretch. Becka sighed contentedly and relaxed in her cushiony bucket seat. Suddenly, with no warning, the sedan in front of Brad braked. Brad, in turn, slammed on his brakes, and Becka stood on hers—but not in time. A deafening metallic, crunching noise and the sound of shattering glass brought both vehicles to an abrupt standstill.

Chapter 12

Roses

A sick, devastating awareness surged through Becka. "Oh, no!" she groaned, quickly undoing her seatbelt and leaping out. Brad reached her where their two cars met in a muddle of crushed trunk, hood, and bumpers. Broken glass lay scattered along the road.

With the sight of her little silver Renault looking so pitifully wounded, Becka's eyes filled with tears. She felt Brad's arm slip around her.

"Are you all right?" he asked anxiously.

"Yes," she replied, trembling. "But our cars—oh, Brad! My poor parents! They really sacrificed to buy this car. Now it's ruined."

"But you're insured," he reminded her.

She shook her head, trying to stop the tears. "My insurance will fix your car, Brad, but not mine. We only had the liability kind."

His arm tightened around her waist, and he tried to sound convincing, "Well, maybe it won't cost too much to replace the hood . . . and the grill . . . and—" Just then he recognized a woman walking toward them. "That's her!" he murmured. "The one who stopped in front of me to make a turn. She didn't even signal. No warning of any kind!"

Becka suddenly became aware of the traffic congestion the accident had caused, the slowing vehicles, the gaping eyes. She wished she could melt inconspicuously into the background.

The next hour felt strangely blurred with phone calls, the Coltons' anxious faces, a tow truck. There was the impossible task of squeezing some of Becka's belongings into Brad's already-packed car. The rest of her things were sent back with the Coltons to store until she could retrieve them later.

When Becka watched her little silver Renault being towed away, her heart felt as if a part of her were being towed away also.

The couple began the trip again, this time in the disfigured Mustang, and for quite a distance, they rode in gloomy silence.

Then Becka's tears began anew. "I'm sorry," she sobbed, feeling embarrassed.

"Brad's going to think I'm a big baby," she thought. "I hardly ever cry!" she explained helplessly. "But I just can't . . . can't . . . "

"Hey!" His hand quickly clasped hers. "You've just experienced a major shock, Becka. It's not every day you have an auto accident, you know. And this one was extra hard because that was your very first car. It's kind of like seeing your best friend hurt."

Becka forced a smile, taking comfort in the fact that Brad understood how she felt. But the tears kept coming, as if they had been dammed up for years and were now tumbling over her own personal spillway.

"I—I've always had such control over m—my life," she stammered. "I've always strived to be the best at whatever I do, whether at school, at work, at church, at home." She looked broodingly at the countryside rushing by, then gritted her teeth. "For a few short seconds I didn't have any control at all when . . . when my car skidded into yours. It didn't matter that my foot shoved the brake to the floor. The car just did as it pleased." She gulped a quick breath of air. "I feel like such a failure."

Brad nodded philosophically. He then used his smattering of knowledge in psychology and religion to comfort her. For hours they talked and talked. Only occasional tears slid down her cheeks now, the harmless kind, like gentle rain after a violent thunderstorm. Becka came to learn that tears were sometimes necessary to clear away the cobwebs of despair. By the time they reached the college Becka felt hollow, drained of all emotion except a lingering sadness.

Her father's happy-go-lucky reaction to the accident didn't surprise her. Nothing could ruffle her dad. He told her to wait for an estimate of the damage before she got excited. "Maybe it's not as bad as it looks."

"It's bad, Dad!"

She could tell by the sound of her mother's voice over the phone that she was crying. Mrs. Bailey repeated, "Praise the Lord!" several times and was happy neither her daughter nor Brad had been hurt. "Cars can be repaired, Sweetheart," she said, "but sometimes people can't."

"But the money, Mom!"

"It'll work out, Becka. God's never let us down in the past. I don't know why He'd start now."

When the repair estimate totalled $2,700, Becka felt dazed. "That's three-hundred dollars *more* than it cost!"

Her mother sounded stunned also. "Well, your father and I will discuss this and get back to you."

At the onset of Labor Day weekend Becka received their surprising decision. "The woods have been shut down because of fire danger," her father said. "Since I can't work anyway, I might as well drive my pickup down to Texas, tow your car home, and fix it myself."

Becka couldn't believe her ears. "But Dad! We're not talking about a little trip into town here. Houston's 2,400 miles away from you!"

"Yep!" he said. "And I haven't had a vacation in years. It's about time for one. Anyway, in the long run, even after spending a couple-hundred dollars on gas for the trip, we'll save lots of money fixing the car ourselves."

Becka heard her mother's voice in the background, "Tell her I'm going to help you drive—straight through."

Leaving Washington State on Saturday night, her parents phoned Becka from the Coltons' house on Tuesday evening. "We'll see you and Brad sometime tomorrow afternoon on our way through your town," her mother promised.

The next day, unable to contain her excitement, Becka spotted the oversized blue-and-white pickup with her wounded car in tow. As soon as her father brought the vehicle to a halt, she rushed to his arms and hugged him tightly. Her mother was next, her eyes scrutinizing both Becka and Brad, apparently assuring herself of no broken bones or cuts.

They spent two hours reminiscing. Becka, sitting across from her father, noticed that his blond hair had thinned somewhat and his sideburns were tinged with gray now. But her dad's glinting blue eyes never changed. All too soon she and Brad were waving them off. "See you at Christmas!" she called.

Over the weeks her father delivered progress reports on her Renault. "It'll be ready by Christmas," he promised, "and it'll look better than new!"

Meanwhile, as her car was slowly being repaired, Becka sensed a repairing of her own spirits. The trauma of the accident was fading. She had plunged back into her studies and had returned to her morning regimen of jogging through the sleepy college town. This was her only quiet time of the day, a time of restoration.

She loved the freshness of morning, the dew misting around her, and how the sun seemed to add a coat of varnish to everything, even brightening the few ramshackle houses along her route.

While running, Becka meditated, sometimes considering her stressful lifestyle. Having been raised to observe the eight natural remedies, she at least adhered to seven of them: she drank lots of water, enjoyed Texas' generous supply of sunshine, jogged almost daily, and breathed the unpolluted country air. She was careful about eating a well-balanced, vegetarian diet and abstained from anything that might harm her body, such as caffeine or alcohol—even other people's cigarette smoke.

The one remedy missing in her life, however, was rest. "I have a choice," she pondered. "I can get average grades and sleep eight hours a night or I can get A's and sleep little." This was a popular topic during her early morning jogging session: her conscience would war against her desire to graduate *summa cum laude* the following year. She tried to soothe her prickly conscience by vowing to ease up during graduate school on her way to a doctorate in English. "Anyway," she rationalized, "no one can really glean the best from a full course at college and get the proper amount of rest." Her life had become a complicated juggling act, and the ball marked "sleep" seemed to get tossed aside too often.

"Impossible!" Becka huffed as she rounded a corner, heading toward the town's miniature shopping mall. "Someday, perhaps, I'll return here to join the faculty. Then I'll have some clout and do something about the mounds of homework." She would teach her students how to balance their lives and keep their health. Maybe a five-year-program instead of four!

The padding of her sneakers against the pavement continued through the mornings of September, and they sometimes splashed through puddles during October. November brought the crunching of autumn leaves at her feet and a crisp breeze around her.

Brad had found a job as a hospital orderly on the graveyard shift a couple of nights a week, and this cut into their time together, most of which was spent studying.

When Sunday, November 20, arrived Brad barely finished typing the body of a term paper before he needed to return to his dorm. "I've got to work tonight," he told Becka, "and I shouldn't report to duty without at least a two-hour nap."

"Go on!" she ordered. "I'll type your title page, end notes, and bibliography."

"Really?"

"Sure! What are friends for, anyway?" she exclaimed. She shooed him out of the college computer center and sat down at a terminal. Two other girls were finishing their term papers as well, so she wasn't alone—until they left at eleven-thirty.

At midnight the printer clattered to a stop and gave up Brad's last page of endnotes. Becka straightened herself from a hunched position over the keys, stretched her weary back muscles, and yawned. Then she returned to the computer terminal, where she began a critical paper for English. She had a good rough draft on the screen by two a.m., something to consult her professor about in the morning before proceeding with the project. But Becka felt too tired to wait for a printout, so she shuffled over to the phone and called Security for an escort back to her building.

When she reached her room and plopped down on the bed, her American Literature book stared accusingly at her. She still had to read a story tonight—*uh, this morning*! "Someday I'll change things," she thought, "but, for now, I read."

She skipped her usual run and slept in till seven-thirty. Hurrying to the computer center, she printed the draft of her critical paper, separated the pages, and stacked them neatly.

A few minutes later, when she rushed past the glassed-in office where she worked part time in the English Department, something bright red registered on her brain. As she raced down the hall, an image of her tall and grinning girlfriend, Laura, also registered belatedly. Laura was grinning at the bright red—roses! Becka instantly reversed her steps, nearly stumbling over her feet.

Her friend laughed. "I was wondering when you'd notice them."

"Oh, they're beautiful!" Becka cried, examining the bouquet that stood in a ceramic blue vase on her desk.

She plucked a card from its center and found Brad's small-ish script on both sides:

Happy anniversary, Darling! One year ago today we enjoyed our first date. Would you go out with me tonight? Same place, only a year later? Love, Brad.

P.S. Thanks so much for finishing the typing on my term paper. I know what a chore that must have been. I really appreciate you, Becka.

"Ooooh!" she swooned, melting into a chair. "Brad is *so* sweet." Then she quickly regained her senses and raced down the hallway to her appointment with the professor.

That evening she and Brad sat amidst candlelight and violin music at "their" restaurant. Somehow, it didn't matter to her that she was running on only a few hours' sleep. Brad had a knack for revitalizing her energy.

Their meal was nearly over when he said, "I've been doing a lot of serious thinking about us lately."

"In what way?"

"Oh, how much we have in common. We both love Jesus.

We share the same kind of goals. We're great friends. That's important, you know."

"Very important," she replied, wondering where this conversation was headed.

"I've really grown to love you, Becka. When I consider my future, I can't imagine it without you in it."

"I've grown to love you too, Brad," she admitted. In fact, Becka couldn't remember a time past Christmas when she didn't love Brad. She had loved him when they played George and Emily in *Our Town*; she had loved him before they started working at El Camino Ranch; she had loved him when he and his father rushed down the hill to fight fire in their good suits; she had loved him when he comforted her after the accident.

Their eyes met in an awkward silence, and, momentarily, the music sounded oddly loud. Brad glanced around the restaurant before he asked, "Becka, what do you think about the possibility of our getting married someday?"

Her heart jumped, sending her pulse into doubletime. Scarcely breathing, she answered, "Well, to be honest, I've often wondered if the Lord Himself arranged for me to go to college so far from home just so I could meet you. You have so many of the qualities I consider important for a husband." She giggled nervously. "And after all, my mother's already ordered me to hold on to you."

"She said that?"

Becka nodded.

"Mmmm!" He reached across the table and held both of her hands in his. "I know we're still in college right now, and it would be impractical to get married before we have some savings stored up. But what do you think about giving our parents notice, so they can start planning now for a grand wedding?"

Becka gazed into his warm brown eyes and replied, "Let's find a phone!"

One love . . .
two uncompromising faiths!

The roar of jet engines, a heavy sigh, and it was done. Jennifer Perkins was on her way to a new life at Newbold College in England.

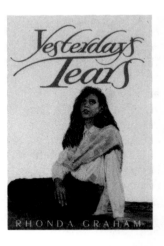

Left behind in the States was Mike, the man she loved. They shared such happiness . . . but she *had* to leave. What future could there be for a young Seventh-day Adventist woman and a Jewish man?

But for Jennifer, the complications increase when Scott enters her life.

From author Rhonda Graham comes **Yesterday's Tears**, a tender love story about Christian convictions, choices, and God's promise never to leave us without support.

US$6.95/Cdn$8.70. 96 pages. Paper.

Please photocopy and complete form below.

- -

❏*Yesterday's Tears*
US$6.95/Cdn$8.70

Please add applicable sales tax and 15% (US$2.50 minimum) to cover postage and handling.

Name _____

Address _____

City _____

State _____ Zip _____

Price	$ _____	Order from your Adventist Book Center, or ABC
Postage	$ _____	Mailing Service, P.O. Box 7000, Boise, Idaho
Sales Tax	$ _____	83707. Prices subject to change without notice.
TOTAL	$ _____	Make check payable to Adventist Book Center.

FAMILY READING
AT ITS BEST!

Now you know Becka. But have you met Hazel? *The Adventures of Hazel Weston*, a four-book series by Paula Montgomery, tells the story of Hazel "Big Enough" Weston—a young cowgirl who grew up in the wilds of eastern Oregon during the early 1900s.

Canyon Girl captures the excitement of Indians, roundups, rattlesnakes, and life for a little girl in the wild West. **228 pages. Paper.**

Valley Girl finds Hazel and her family trapped in the worst snowstorm of the century. Only Hazel can go for help! **180 pages. Paper.**

A great drought overshadows Hazel's high-school days in *Hood River Girl.* Forests explode into flame and plunge the Columbia River Gorge into smokey darkness. **174 pages. Paper.**

In Grandma's Footsteps traces Hazel's experiences in nurse's training—exotic patients, clowning dormmates, and even a mysterious prowler. **156 pages. Paper.**

Before Becka, there was Hazel. Get *The Adventures of Hazel Weston* series today!

US$24.95/Cdn$31.20 for set of four books.

Please photocopy and complete the form below.